# Praise for *Trapped in the Present T...*

"A collection of light-footed philosophic... out parallels between the lives of famed... als who led 'lowercase lives.'"    —R...

"Evocative . . . Whether it's gun violence, ...uclear war or government incursions on Americans' privacy, Brooks's concerns are broad and vital . . . Colette Brooks cogently assesses an array of modern American problems through the lens of history and recollection."

—*Shelf Awareness*

"This is a sophisticated, thoughtful collection that should be read with the kind of care that Brooks instilled into each provocative essay."

—*Booklist*

"What is a memory? Colette Brooks searchingly explores this question, one so fundamental we never really ask it, to uncover the sinuous paths by which public and private information intersect and mutate to form something quite separate from events as they occurred. Brooks doesn't merely describe but rather enacts this process. In prose that moves between urgent, reflective, and intimate registers, she makes vivid how the news—in all its evolving but always insistent forms—has colonized our most intimate selves. *Trapped in the Present Tense* charts this new consciousness and takes astute stock of its social and emotional implications."    —Albert Mobilio, author of *Same Faces*

"One of the pleasures of reading Colette Brooks is relinquishing what I thought I knew about her subjects. The startling clarity of her thinking, the lucidity of her sentences, and her knack for knowing where to look transform whatever she's writing about into something strangely unfamiliar and thrilling. And in *Trapped in the Present Tense*, Brooks reveals the contemporary moment to be both mournfully inevitable and utterly unexpected."    —Alex Halberstadt, author of *Young Heroes of the Soviet Union*

ALSO BY COLETTE BROOKS

*Lost in Wonder: Imagining Science and Other Mysteries*
*In the City: Random Acts of Awareness*

# TRAPPED
## *in the*
# PRESENT TENSE

*Meditations on American Memory*

## Colette Brooks

COUNTERPOINT
California

Trapped in the Present Tense

Copyright © 2022 by Colette Brooks

First Counterpoint edition: 2022
First paperback edition: 2024

All rights reserved under domestic and international copyright. Outside of fair use (such as quoting within a book review), no part of this publication may be reproduced, stored in a retrieval system, or transmitted in any form or by any means, electronic, mechanical, photocopying, recording, or otherwise, without the written permission of the publisher. For permissions, please contact the publisher.

The Library of Congress has cataloged the hardcover edition as follows:
Names: Brooks, Colette, author.
Title: Trapped in the present tense : meditations on American memory / Colette Brooks.
Description: First hardcover edition. | Berkeley, California : Counterpoint, 2021.
Identifiers: LCCN 2020053899 | ISBN 9781640093324 (hardcover) | ISBN 9781640093331 (ebook)
Subjects: LCSH: National characteristics, American. | Memory—Social aspects—United States. | Collective memory—United States. | United States—Civilization—1945–
Classification: LCC E169.12 .B723 2021 | DDC 973—dc23
LC record available at https://lccn.loc.gov/2020053899

Paperback ISBN: 978-1-64009-563-2

Cover design by Dana Li
Book design by Jordan Koluch

COUNTERPOINT
Los Angeles and San Francisco, CA
www.counterpointpress.com

Printed in the United States of America

10 9 8 7 6 5 4 3 2 1

For Charlotte French Brooks and Devon

# Contents

*Trapped in the Present Tense*

# PREFACE

*A person born in the mid-twentieth century might be forgiven for trying to live an analog life, hoping to hold on to memory, even as the act of remembering itself slips into cultural obsolescence.*

*It isn't easy.*

*In the twenty-first century, even the most reflective among us seem to be trapped in the present tense, events superseded so rapidly that awareness can hardly keep up. No before or after anymore, just here and now, 24/7.*

*Like Zen moments without the mindfulness.*

*In such a cultural shift, when concepts of past and future are losing their currency, familiar expressions fail as well: 'one thing after another,' 'ask me later,' 'someday you'll understand,' 'the long arc of justice' make less and less sense, as if language itself is faltering.*

*On an individual level one can adapt; it might even be liberating to cast aside complex notions like hope or regret. But on a national level the loss of connection does more damage. We lose the capacity to place experience in a larger framework, and without that ability, we have little to cushion the shocks that keep coming.*

*Those of us who have witnessed bits and pieces of what we still call the past—however narrow our perspective—have an opportunity, if not an obligation, to place a marker down, to remember.*

*It's worth a shot.*

*And so, as oblivion approaches, it may be time to go old school, to tell stories that slow the acceleration down, to practice acts of true attention. In this way, we might keep alive one of the only old questions that still matters:*

*How did all this happen?*

# Shooters

*As of 2019, every American could be given a gun and there would still be 67 million guns at large in every nook and cranny of the country. That's 393 million weapons stored in homes, tossed in alleys, sold in shops, stolen, or passed along to family members at any given moment.*

*Few actually know how a gun works, that projectiles in its chambers are driven by a rapidly expanding high-pressure gas produced by exothermic combustion and then ejected.*

*You wouldn't want to get in the way of a projectile.*

*You wouldn't want to be caught in the cross fire, look down the barrel, bite the bullet, jump the gun, take a cheap shot, or lower your sights.*

*You might want to stick to your guns, keep your powder dry, dodge a bullet, find a smoking gun, pull the trigger, or go out with guns blazing, depending on the situation.*

*You could be characterized by others as a big shot, or, alternately, a son of a gun.*

*But it never hurts to be considered a straight shooter.*

*It's almost impossible to imagine living in a culture that isn't saturated in such imagery, but there was a time when most Americans had other things on their minds.*

*And there was nothing routine about being shot at.*

# I

*Instead of tranquilizers, why not try an ocean trip? When you walk off the gangplank in Europe, you'll probably throw your pills away.*
—Advertisement, *The New York Times,*
August 2, 1966

1966 is something of a liminal year in American life; it isn't yet 1968, with cultural fault lines fully developed, but schisms have begun to appear in a restive nation increasingly at odds with itself. There's a war on, but many people still support it; the country has survived a traumatic assassination, but doesn't yet know that others are soon to follow. "Ballad of the Green Berets" by Sgt. Barry Sadler, an upbeat Vietnam anthem, sits at the top of the pop charts for five weeks; an edgier tune, "Wild Thing," vies with "Good Vibrations" for airtime, while Simon and Garfunkel (*Hello darkness, my old friend*) introduce a mainstream audience to melancholy.

During one week in late summer, newspaper accounts report that Dr. Martin Luther King Jr., who has two years yet to live, has implored police to protect civil rights marchers in the Midwest; B-52 bombers have dropped tons of ordnance on suspected Vietcong outside Saigon, but ground troops can't find any bodies; in Chicago Richard Speck, a young man described as *a drifter*, pleads not guilty at his arraignment for the murder of eight nurses; and Luci Baines Johnson, daughter of the president, gets a $2,000 tea set at a posh engagement party in Washington hosted by Ambassador W. Averell Harriman.

So far, business as usual.

But on a ninety-eight-degree day shortly before noon the usual is interrupted, abruptly, as a lone sniper climbs a tower at the University of Texas, Austin, and begins to shoot.

August 1, 1966: a day that will seem utterly unforgettable in American life, until it fades from the memory of all but a few.


Charles Whitman, a twenty-five-year-old architectural engineering student, has assembled an array of weapons for his work, the kind that will later be termed *an arsenal*. He's got three rifles (with one, a Remington 700 6mm bolt-action with a telescopic sight, he can take down a target at 1,500 feet), a 12-gauge semiautomatic shotgun (bought on credit from Sears), a 9mm Luger, and a .357 Magnum pistol he had once tried to sell to a friend. Later, police also find a knife, a low-tech fallback for close-range encounters. It might be the one he used to kill his wife and mother shortly after midnight.

Whitman has also packed other provisions: his military-issue footlocker contains water, sandwiches, Dexedrine, ammo, toiletries, and a transistor radio. His perch two hundred some feet above campus offers sweeping perspectives with excellent sight lines all around. He knows the territory; he's visited the tower's observation deck twice with friends and family in recent months, which suggests if nothing else that he's probably a planner. He also has the element of surprise, which will quickly turn to shock. And shock is disorienting, which he can use to his advantage.

No one will be as well prepared as he is for what happens on this day.

For the next ninety minutes the quiet college town is transfixed as the first modern mass shooting in America unfolds.

Students walking across campus are slow to take it seriously, the bodies seem to crumple in some kind of strangely orchestrated synchronization. Some think it's the work of a theater group, or a psychology class experiment. For others on the street, who don't think much about college life anymore, it's all too real. Pedestrians scatter and drivers abandon cars, doors open and engines running, in the middle of the road.

There doesn't seem to be anywhere to hide. He shoots a boy off a bicycle hundreds of yards away. He hits people who have crouched behind thin barriers or windows. He hits others who are running (no one's walking anymore). He hits men and women, young and middle-aged indiscriminately. One student, looking through binoculars, lenses glinting in the sun, sees the barrel of the rifle swing straight at him and seconds later feels the projectile *whoosh* just above his head.

He pulls the trigger over fifty times.

Eventually, the casualty count rises to sixteen killed, thirty-three wounded. Whitman's own demise, the only *justifiable homicide* of the day, will raise the death toll to seventeen, though officials are ambivalent about formally acknowledging it in any way.

The *accident*, as it will later be known in Austin, will eventually be ended by just two cops and a hastily deputized civilian who scramble to the top of the tower. They won't have much in the way of a plan; no police department has yet had to cope with random murder, someone just taking shots at strangers, armed with weaponry against which police-issue pistols seem comically ineffectual. They don't have radios and the phone lines are down. There's no useful precedent for how to proceed. (Sheriff Andy and his sidekick Barney Fife, from the mythical TV town of Mayberry, are possibly the most well-known lawmen in America, and nothing like this has ever happened to them.) They haven't got any real protection, either, no Kevlar vests or shields. But if they sneak up on the shooter, rush him, empty every gun they've got, maybe they can overwhelm him.

At this point they don't know anything about him, except that he's a much better shot than they are.

By now civilians on the ground, some of them students, are shooting wildly upward with rifles of their own that they've grabbed. A pilot circles the tower in a small plane and takes some shots out his window as well. Nothing comes close, but the distraction gives the two cops on-site an opening.

Finally, after what may be the longest hour and a half in Austin history, the Remington 700 is silenced.

The entire situation will seem impossibly primitive to later experts in law enforcement. It will, however, spur the formation of a new kind of rapid response team, SWAT, a paramilitary force with enough training and firepower to ensure that no cop ever feels so outgunned again.

Days later, the rest of the world will wonder about what's gone wrong in the States. A London paper marvels that 750,000 Americans have been killed by guns since 1900, more dead than in all its foreign wars. Another notes that *sudden violence is familiar in America*. The curiosity is genuine, not yet rhetorical. From a distance, it's difficult to fathom the gawky, often brutal nation that isn't given to introspection. Maybe this event will lead to some kind of understanding.

Everyone wants to know why, including the shooter himself. He's left a couple of notes (*To Whom It May Concern*). *I don't really understand myself these days . . . I have been a victim of many unusual and irrational thoughts.* It must be maddening to find oneself at the mercy of some mysterious urging, deep and constant. He sees himself as under siege. He mentions headaches. He asks for an autopsy, maybe it will provide answers.

He wants the world to know that he cared for his wife, and always tried to protect his mother. *I loved that woman with all my heart* (he adds the word *all* in an edit, he wants no misunderstanding). The note writing is interrupted by friends, who will say, after their visit, that he seemed calm, as if he had finally solved a problem.

Later that evening he resumes writing. Just the facts now. *Interrupted. 3 am: Both Dead.*

It isn't just his family that he thinks about on this last night of his life. He has something to say about society as well: *I truly do not consider this world worth living in.*

Whitman's own words, though interesting, are anecdotal. A deeper explanation will require a more dispassionate examination of the evidence.

Twenty-three scientific specialists are asked to collaborate on a report commissioned by Governor John Connally. The group is comprised of professionals in neuropathology, the psychopathic personality, tumors, and the microscopic anatomy of the brain. An expert in psychiatric problems associated with acts of violence is also asked to weigh in.

If there's anything determinative to be found, the thinking goes, these fellows will find it.

But there's only so much a brain resection can reveal. The science of tissue study says nothing about the power of those thoughts he'd been having, how the sight of animate specks moving far below him might be mesmerizing. Or how the view from that tower could become, arguably, an obsession operating at a level much deeper than a diagnosis.


The commission's primary charge is the "collection of all medical facts" relating to what is formally decreed *The Charles J. Whitman Catastrophe*. In the mid-1960s, such an event is rare enough that it seems appropriate to personalize it. In future, more general designations such as Columbine or Aurora or Virginia Tech or Sandy Hook will serve, like placeholders, to punctuate the flood of *active shooter incidents* that have become commonplace in American life.

The report draws upon other sources of information: 'all available written material'—police, service, and school records; diaries, letters, and interviews with friends. It contains an important caveat: *the information is not exhaustive and all encompassing.* That's an ambition that wildly exceeds current capabilities.

They learn that Whitman was, on paper, exemplary: an Eagle Scout, altar boy, dorm counselor, and Marine sharpshooter who spent his tour stationed in the tropics (no war trauma there). He had a modest criminal record – a bounced check in 1962, traffic tickets in 1966. There was also some trouble in the service. Friends further cite a few "way out ideas," including atheism, but most people liked him even so. He was *Charlie*, a good kid, a great guy, meticulous, ambitious, in many ways even admirable. There's no hint of anything awry in the photographs: in school portraits of the mid-sixties the boys still have crew cuts, suits and ties, and Whitman's got the kind of bland good looks that seem to portend a bright future in the Rotary Club. He's not a dropout, or a drifter, the two types that usually spell trouble.

They look next at the family, especially the father, a gun collector who runs a small business in Florida. He expresses shock at the incident, but he can vouch for the technique. *Charlie*, he says, *could plug the eye out of a squirrel by the time he was sixteen.* He should know; he taught the boy how to hunt.

He's surprised that his son hated him, something he learns from several sources after the fact. It's outrageous, but there's an explanation. Yes, he was strict, he sometimes hit his wife, she finally left him, but he was trying to get her back. He has two other sons who are fine. What happened isn't his fault. He now realizes, as everyone else should, that his oldest son was *sick*.

The report includes a perfunctory account of the only known visit Whitman ever made to a psychiatrist, a university therapist he saw for an hour earlier that year. The notes begin with a few first impressions. This new patient is a *massive, muscular youth oozing with hostility.* By his own admission something is happening

to him, but he isn't articulate about what it might be, except perhaps when he speaks of *going up on the tower with a deer rifle and
shooting people.* That's fairly specific, memorable enough to put in
quotation marks. (Later, a classmate will remember that he made a
similar comment years earlier.) But it won't prompt any particular
follow-up, possibly because no one in a quiet college town in 1966
can imagine a twenty-five-year old, hostile or not, behaving in such
a manner. However the doctor will be happy to talk with the young
man again, provided he makes an appointment.

Whitman will never return, but the encounter will spur future
debate about just what constitutes a *warning sign.*


A pecan-sized tumor is subsequently found in Whitman's head, but
nobody thinks it's conclusive. *Existing knowledge of organic brain
function does not enable us to explain the actions of Whitman on
August 1.* At most it might be contributory. Beyond the lack of reliable science, it just doesn't seem enough to explain actions that most
people consider evil.

An FBI profiler, decades later, will dismiss the tumor theory as
well. She's studied the Whitman case and has a simpler explanation.
It's the fruit of twenty-eight years of experience. She doesn't think
such killers snap because of a medical condition. That's too easy.

Some people, she believes, just have a natural drive to kill, and
Charles Whitman was one of them.

Over time the Whitman catastrophe will recede in memory for
most Americans. But one man will think about chance and fate for
the rest of his life. It's a story he could tell in his sleep. He was a UT
undergraduate in 1966, with a registrar's appointment on August
1 at noon, the moment the shooting began. He would have been
ambling into the gunsights himself that day if his usually punctual

roommate, the one with the car, hadn't been late, late enough so that he missed everything but the aftermath.

Fifty years on, he still hasn't heard a convincing explanation for what happened. But he has developed a deep awareness of how such an experience can radiate far beyond those immediately affected, the ones in the casualty counts. He doesn't need a report to remind him of that. It's something that's shadowed him ever since. He might be speaking for many whose thoughts dwell on such a day.

*Even if you avoid harm's way, these can be haunting events.*

# 2

The Whitman commission, in passing, questions the growing presence of violence in news and entertainment programming. The observation is clearly aimed at television, that relatively new medium, *the box*, that Americans are still learning how to live with. The commission's reference is oblique; it doesn't mention that the entire country watched as the assassination of a president was covered on live TV just three years earlier, a spectacle that mesmerized the public. Who knows what effect such sights could have on people, the kind of people who shouldn't be watching such stuff. *Acts of violence and tragedy are given prominence in all news media, accessible to young as well as old.* To anyone, in fact, who can turn on the TV.

No wonder they'd like to put the genie back in the bottle.

Rewind to 1963: viewers have just three television channels to choose from. The nightly national news broadcasts, aired punctually at the dinner hour, have recently been expanded from fifteen to thirty minutes. They immerse viewers in a grainy black-and-white world with a single fixed camera framing dour men behind a desk. But the images exert an undeniable hold on the public.

Entertainment shows like *Father Knows Best* help to usher in the new era. The Andersons—America's favorite TV family—are impossibly serene residents of Springfield, a city without discernible racial, ethnic, or class tensions. Jim sells insurance, Margaret holds sway in the house, *the children* get into and out of jams that their parents adjudicate with a warm ease each week. Bud needs help organizing a school picnic, Kathy's nervous about the county spelling contest, Margaret suspects that Betty may have taken part in a prank.

Outside the home a nascent civil rights movement may be building, other varieties of social and political turmoil may be brewing, but here, for thirty minutes, viewers experience a reassuring focus on the uneventful course of ordinary life.

A generation later another iconic American family, the Simpsons, will themselves reside in Springfield, a sly homage for those old enough to recognize the reference. By that time one of the child actors of *Father Knows Best*, as an adult, will have offered an apology to viewers for having promoted a false vision of life on the show, but his *mea culpa* will be roundly rejected by an avid fan base that isn't much interested in revisionism. Fans also won't want to know that Robert Young, the actor who played Jim, battled alcoholism and thoughts of suicide when off the set.

They're only interested in the uncomplicated fantasy figures they once welcomed into their homes.

While shows like *Father Knows Best* provide wholesome fare for an evening's entertainment, television in the early 1960s offers a darker glimpse of American life during the daytime hours, when the family is dispersed (women in the house, men at work, children in school). Homemakers and other shut-ins are then free to follow the dystopian ups and downs of adult characters whose struggles can't be resolved in thirty minutes, but unravel fitfully over months and sometimes years, much like the meandering of their own lives.

On one late November day in 1963 viewers are likely to be watching a live broadcast of *As the World Turns*, the number one daytime program in the nation (it will run for fifty-four years before it finally ends). The show opens with an organ flourish and cuts to a commercial for Niagara starch, possessor of the Good Housekeeping Seal. That still means something in a 1960s supermarket.

Like many Americans, the Hughes family is thinking about Thanksgiving. As the drama begins, its middle-aged matriarch, Nancy, is knitting a holiday sweater for the grandson she sees less than she'd like because things aren't resolved between his divorced parents. (Viewers know that she doesn't blame her son Bob, but lately he's been moody and that doesn't bode well for the upcoming holidays.) Over the next several minutes Nancy will learn that Bob has impulsively invited his ex to Thanksgiving dinner, an action that mystifies her, and a conversation with Grandpa over coffee won't clear anything up.

Because it's a live broadcast the actors occasionally muff their lines, the stumbles slowing them up so that they seem to be groping for words, lending their strained efforts to communicate a kind of unintended gravitas so that nothing, it seems, is more urgent at this moment than the possibility of a rapprochement between Lisa and Bob.

Ten minutes into the program no one's thinking about the Hughes family anymore.

A message announcing a CBS News Bulletin appears on-screen and viewers hear the avuncular voice of newsman Walter Cronkite as he attempts to get their attention. (He knows they can't see him.) Cronkite is a recently appointed news anchor; in nine years he'll be voted the most trusted man in America, thanks in part to the connection he makes to the television audience over the next several days.

Chaotic reports have begun to stream onto the news wires— shots have been fired at the presidential motorcade in Dallas; the president is alive, or he might be dead, there's a gunman in a building, or a man and woman with weapons on a hillside, Mrs. Kennedy was heard to say *oh no*, or she didn't say anything, someone has seen a priest, someone else saw two, the Vice President is at the hospital, or he's been whisked away.

Viewers are urged to stay tuned for further details as they develop.

The network switches to a commercial for instant coffee, which runs in its entirety, after which viewers are shown a blank screen, then the spinning globe signaling the resumption of *As the World Turns*. A dramatic scene with Bob at lunch in a restaurant ensues (he's talking about someone named Penny now); it's followed by a commercial for dog food.

Then, abruptly, the blank screen reappears.

The jumpiness seems to mirror the newly unsettled state of the national psyche.


No one in the control room knows how to handle the situation, there are no guidelines for covering a seismic story that's unfolding in real time; the news has always been neatly relegated to its regularly scheduled period at the end of the day.

Cronkite, working on instinct, calls for a live studio shot. It will take several long minutes before the camera warms up. In the meantime, viewers effectively experience a reversion to radio as the TV audience (listening to the anchor off camera) sees only the now ominous CBS News Bulletin announcement on the screen. Cronkite fills some of the time by recalling the particulars of attacks upon other presidents—Harry Truman in 1950 (Puerto Rican separatists), FDR's near miss in Florida even earlier.

Everyone is waiting, the newsmen don't know any more than those watching about what's happening.

Once the picture is up it reveals a newsroom in disarray, staffers on the run ripping pages from teletypes as they arrive. Cronkite is at a makeshift desk, in shirtsleeves, glancing at notes thrust at him from off-screen. Reports about the president's condition are rushing in, most of them dire but none definitive.

At 2:38 p.m. EST another wire report arrives and Cronkite announces, finally, that the President is dead.

He takes off his glasses. He seems to be struggling to maintain his composure. It's a simple gesture that will become a touchstone in the evolution of broadcast television, a moment when the emotion of millions was expressed by the one man they were all watching.

For the next several days regular programming is preempted as the three networks focus on the events in Dallas and their aftermath, culminating in live shots of the state funeral in Washington. The saturation coverage is unprecedented; no story has ever been followed on such a scale with such immediacy. Most of those who own TVs are thought to have tuned in at some point.

No one knows if twenty-two-year-old Charles Whitman was watching, but almost everyone else would have been, hardly able to turn away, the horror creeping into their homes but still at some remove. They still feel safe.

*I'm not the president, that would never happen to me.*

It's almost reassuring.

Viewers are drawn to the suspected assassin, taken into custody shortly after the shooting and held for the moment in makeshift circumstances at the Dallas City Jail. It's a kind of venomous attention that some may never have felt before. Through the live TV feed of the local network affiliate they catch glimpses of him whenever he's shuffled from one room or floor to another. He's ordinary looking, on the short side, scrawny, the kind of fellow who wouldn't turn heads in any other circumstance. But a national audience is watching him now.

Over time Lee Oswald, a nobody, will morph into *Lee Harvey Oswald*, a mythic figure in American life, but at this point he still seems almost vanishingly small on the screen.

On the morning of the 24th, two days after the assassination,

Oswald is scheduled to be taken from the city jail to county facilities. Cops and reporters in Stetsons crowd the basement corridor, jostling for a vantage point (the TV camera's got the best view, and those who stand unthinkingly in front of it are brusquely pushed aside). The transfer is fairly straightforward, but just to be safe police have brought in an armored truck to move the suspect. As it turns out, they won't need it; five seconds after Oswald swings into view, a moment after someone shouts *there he is*, a single shot rings out and he's down.

Everyone is jostling now.

The iconic shot that will forever fix the moment is taken by a print photographer, but the visceral feeling of the event is captured in a new way by television.

The TV camera is so close it seems like viewers are right there in the cramped space.

They hear the last conscious utterance Oswald will ever make, something that sounds like surprise, as he grabs his gut and collapses onto the concrete. The man who shot him is later identified as the owner of a Dallas nightclub. He, like Oswald, will eventually be ruled a lone gunman, though those findings will always be disputed.

It's hard to believe that a single man could act to such devastating effect.

The TV newsman on the scene is just as stunned as everyone else but he has to say something. He turns to the camera and improvises.

*He's been shot. Lee Oswald has been shot. Absolute panic. Absolute panic here in the basement of the Dallas Police Headquarters.*

But the commentary can't possibly compete with the pictures, it's merely a confirmation of what shaken viewers have just seen with their own eyes. It's not even news anymore, it's something else, a new kind of entertainment, an unexpected irruption of reality into living rooms across the nation. Some watching may have wished they'd pulled the trigger themselves.

For many that jolt won't easily be forgotten. It might even be missed as regular programming resumes.

Another shooter of a different sort will make his own history that week.

On the morning of the 22nd businessman Abraham Zapruder is just another bystander waiting for the presidential motorcade outside the Texas School Book Depository; by late afternoon, he'll be a person of extraordinary interest to historians and future conspiracy theorists of all stripes. On this occasion he hopes to capture a piece of history for his grandchildren. The twenty-six-second motorcade sequence he shoots with his brand-new Bell & Howell 8mm movie camera will prove to be a home movie unlike any other, the most complete record of the assassination available from any source.

Zapruder's film has to be processed in a lab, a procedure that takes some time. (The ubiquity of smartphones and the instant transmission of their images is fifty some years in the future.) He's got a sickening feeling about it, he knows what he saw, but he can't really be sure what's there until the finished footage is run through a projector.

In decades to come, the 486 frames of the film he shot will be picked apart, blown up, screened in slow motion, projected against various time codes, and interrogated from every conceivable angle, but on first viewing it seems fairly straightforward. For 200-some frames the motorcade glides slowly down Elm, the president and Jackie waving to the crowds, office workers, families, and children waving back; at frame 228 the president seems to clutch his throat; a moment later the limo is in front of Zapruder, dead center, as the president slumps into his seat.

At frame 371 Jackie crawls onto the trunk of the moving car; at frame 388 a Secret Service agent pushes her back.

Zapruder keeps shooting, his zoom lens locked on to the car until it disappears. Later that day, after he's absorbed some of the shock, he'll realize, with a shudder, how close he was to the action.

*I must have been in the line of fire.*

He doesn't yet know that a new world is dawning, one his footage is helping to create, where everyone, at some point, will feel like they're in the line of fire.

For some time after the assassination he has nightmares. Every night he sees the sequence, it plays over and over in his head like it's on some kind of loop. Whenever he's asked about his experience he can hardly speak. He'll never be able to describe what he saw except in the most hesitant manner. It—*the thing*—was *tragic, awful, terrible, terrible.* He's always polite, but words can't begin to convey what he feels.

*I loved the President, and to see that happen before my eyes . . .*
He can't finish the sentence. The film will have to speak for him.

Zapruder sells the rights to *Life* magazine for $150,000, a small fortune in 1963. (He wants to serve the public interest, but he's still a businessman.) There's one shot the public won't be allowed to see; it's excised from the sequence *Life* prints that week. It's frame 313, the infamous head shot, the one that shows an explosive pink mist, disturbing even decades later, and the wound that made the rush to the hospital moot. It's deemed too graphic for general consumption by *Life* executives, and it makes Zapruder himself queasy. In 1964 *Life* will finally print the frame. The film itself will be shown to the public for the first time in 1975 when showman Geraldo Rivera screens a bootleg version on TV. In the more distant future, Kennedy autopsy photos will be accessible on the Internet. By then most everyone will realize that no image, once captured on camera, can be suppressed forever.

His Bell & Howell camera will eventually be placed on display in the National Archives, and his heirs will be paid $16 million for the original film. It's considered a landmark artifact in American history.

Zapruder himself may have the last halting word on that history, a kind of impromptu meditation on how anyone's life can unravel, without warning, a fine fall day darkening until everything seems *terrible* and there's no turning back. It's one of the few moments when he knows exactly what he wants to say.

*I wish this would never have happened.*

Official records of the assassination will be embargoed in the National Archives for fifty-four years, but time won't dim the intensity of the public's interest in the event. In 2017 a thousand people comment online in *The Washington Post* after the new material is released. Most of them had hoped for resolution, but experience a now familiar frustration.

*We'll never get the real story in our lifetimes. I give up.*

Meanwhile, someone in New York City propounds another theory, scrawled in black ink on a lamppost.

*Jackie killed JFK.*

It seems a stretch, but given enough time someone is bound to believe it.

# 3

Though Charles Whitman had a large collection of weapons in his possession, there is no mention in the 1966 postmortem of a need to restrict access to firearms (the idea of gun control hasn't yet coalesced into the periodic call to arms it will later become in American life). Commission members do, however, seem concerned about the possibility of former soldiers like Whitman roving the streets, young men with too much time on their hands and a lethal skill set that may not easily translate to civilian life. But at this early juncture, when things aren't yet FUBAR, they can put a positive gloss on the problem.

*It is believed possible for military personnel who have been trained to kill to re-learn in such a way as to de-emphasize in their minds those hostile acts taught as laudatory in time of war.*

Whitman's own service transpired on the American military base at Guantánamo, Cuba, where he combated, at worst, bouts of boredom punctuated by some card-sharking. He would appear to be the epitome of a one-off. But it may be that Whitman is considered the canary in the coal mine. The real specter haunting this section of the report seems to be the conflict developing in the tiny country of Vietnam, a place halfway across the world that most Americans, if put to the test, couldn't get to within a thousand miles of on a map. In 1966 some 385,000 American soldiers will be posted in Vietnam, most of them swept up in a draft that's just doubled to 35,000 notices per month. By year's end over a million Americans will have been *in-country* for at least one twelve-month tour. That's long enough to do some serious wondering, like just what the heck Americans are doing in an Asian land war anyway.

Thoughts like that can poison an attitude, and even filter back to the folks at home.

A boosterish government film of the period is preemptively aimed at popular opinion: *Soldiers serving in Vietnam spend little time analyzing the war, for they are too busy fighting it.*

In other words, the grunts on the ground aren't overthinking it, and Americans sitting stateside on comfortable couches shouldn't either.


Everyone needs to be educated.

It's a new kind of war, nothing like the conflicts one's father or grandfathers fought; here there are battlefields without boundaries, and the enemy (*Charlie, gooks, little men in black pajamas*) is indistinguishable from the civilian population, able to melt into the countryside or villages at will. The nimbleness and resilience of the foe are captured in a new phrase in popular usage, *guerrilla warfare*, useful for those who have forgotten how American colonists defeated their British occupiers during the Revolution. And there are visual aids to ease the transition into the new era.

For the first time, it's war *as seen on TV.*

Fifty million feet of combat footage was shot in World War II, but audiences watched the short newsreel clips at their neighborhood movie theaters. Now, they have daily front-row seats in their own homes (the last newsreel company will be driven out of business in 1967). Battlefield access is unrestricted; reporters and network correspondents move about the Vietnamese countryside at will, hitching rides on helicopters known as Hueys, the latest in utility transport. Their film is airlifted to the States for development and broadcast a day later, on the network newscasts, or published a week later in magazines like *Life*.

The military doesn't censor news reports. Even the flag-draped coffins coming home are unloaded on national television.

That's a mistake that won't be repeated in future conflicts.

The national news broadcasts begin to showcase daily segments on the war. Newscasters, sitting in front of large maps of Vietnam, measure progress with a new metric, *the body count*, supplied by the military; the kill ratio always greatly favors the American forces. (It's a tactic that will reappear in a later period of American life, when triumphant announcements of the death of another *Al-Qaeda leader #3* or *ISIS second-in-command* occur with regularity.) The numbers are meant to make a case for hanging on, success is in sight.

It won't matter that an enemy leader has openly declared *you can kill ten of my men for every one I kill of yours, and at that rate, I will still triumph.*

That's got to be a bluff.

The daily newscasts are supplemented by government-produced broadcasts on weekly series like *The Big Picture*. Many of these programs are hosted by tight-lipped actors who are known to the public for playing fictionalized authority figures. The transference is crude but effective in this new medium, where war can be pitched as easily as any other product (particularly if one employs maps and pointers). Viewers are tutored by James Arness (Sheriff Matt Dillon), Jack Webb (Sgt. Joe Friday), Charlton Heston (Moses), and John Wayne, the most celebrated actor-American of all. The public has watched Wayne fight for his country in over two hundred films. He's served in the Revolutionary War, the Western Territories, the Civil War, and World War II; he was at the Alamo, Pearl Harbor, Iwo Jima, and Bataan. In 1968, he'll show up in Vietnam in *The Green Berets*.

Wayne wears combat fatigues in his TV testimonial. His laconic pitch to the public, carefully scripted, can be paraphrased in two words: *Toughen up.*

No one said it would be easy, but it's important.

The programs have to strike the proper balance; viewers need to be reminded of the risk—*the jungle is never safe*—but also the challenge. American soldiers have a job to do. A war to win. It's workmanlike language, usually amped up to an affecting final flourish.

*If freedom is to survive in any American home it must be preserved in such places as South Vietnam.*

Along with inspiration, viewers are given some basic instruction.

There's North Vietnam (communist) and South Vietnam (not communist); an analogy involving dominoes, American values, and, always, *freedom*. There's a dangerously charismatic North Vietnamese leader named Ho Chi Minh, loosely translated as He Who Enlightens. Viewers are not told that Ho corresponded with Presidents Truman, Eisenhower, and Kennedy back in the day, or that he framed his own country's declaration of independence on the American model (*life, liberty and the pursuit of happiness*), traveled the world as a messboy on ocean liners, loves Paris, likes New York, worked in London for the chef Escoffier, and is an ardent nationalist who wants foreign powers to leave his country alone.

All the public needs to know is that he's a communist.

Ho has warned anyone who will listen that colonialism has run its course: *The white man is finished in Asia.*

But what else would a communist be expected to say?


Behind the scenes a more nuanced debate is unfolding at the highest levels on the pros and cons of American involvement in Vietnam. Yes, the French were run out of Vietnam, but America is different, we can win, we have to make it work. National prestige is at stake, as well as the perception of American power. What it means *to win* is not clearly defined.

A couple of skeptics agree with Ho: *No one has demonstrated that a white ground force of whatever size can win a guerrilla war which is at the same time a civil war between Asians.* They are ambivalent, even anguished, they see only folly in moving forward. But it's like yelling fire in an empty theater. No one else is alarmed.

The contentious debate is *eyes only*, and will be kept from the American public until whistleblower Daniel Ellsberg releases the Pentagon Papers in 1971.

Officially, the conflict is uncomplicated.


Not everybody is buying the official version of events. Hippies in embryonic peace marches wave makeshift signs (*Peace Now, America is the Black Man's Battlefield*) and are sometimes jeered by ordinary people passing by. Even the comedian Bob Hope—known for his upbeat Christmas visits to the troops during the Second World

War—has to pivot to accommodate a war that isn't universally popular. The sixty-two-year-old comes up with a new joke for the GIs:
*The draft board burned my draft card.*

In 1966, when eighteen-year-olds have begun to burn their own
draft cards in public protests, that's funny.

In time, the descriptor *living room war* will become a cliché, but in
the mid-sixties it's still fresh. Everyone's watching—the American
public, Europeans, even the other side. The insistent images float
into one's head; it doesn't matter that there isn't much actual shooting in the coverage, it's the general wash, war as a backdrop to one's
daily life.

It's not *over there* anymore, as earlier wars were; it's right here,
right now, *tune in, tune out,* the war will still be here when you
come back.

This kind of reflexive spectatorship will create, over a generation
or two, an American culture that is essentially inured to faraway
wars, even as they extend over five, ten, fifteen years, in distant
places like *Anwar, Kandahar, Tora Bora, Raqqa, Mosul, or Aleppo,*
with *Sunni, Shia, Kurds, Wahhabi, Al-Qaeda,* and such. No one
but foreign correspondents will attempt to keep it all straight.

But in the 1960s, the public is still curious about places like
*Hue, Da Nang, Dak To, Khe Sanh.*

It's not Omaha Beach, for sure, but people are trying to pay
attention.

General Vo Nguyen Giap, architect of the North Vietnamese
victories over the French and the United States, will explain later,
for posterity, that the Vietcong consciously fought on two fronts, in
the cities and villages of South Vietnam, and in American homes.

The Smithsonian National Museum of American History will eventually create an installation on Vietnam, its centerpiece a plastic-covered sofa facing a bank of small TV screens on which the war plays out in endless loops. Visitors can watch Walter Cronkite report from the field in Vietnam and, back in the studio, declare *We are mired in stalemate* over and over again. They can read what a rueful President Lyndon Johnson remarked, privately, after he had watched the reporting on his own TV.

*If I've lost Cronkite, I've lost the country.*

One of the lower-tech Vietnam relics on view is less flashy than multiple TV monitors. It's a Zippo lighter, once carried by an ordinary soldier, unnamed, and now suspended in a Plexiglas cube like something from the Pleistocene. During the war the ubiquitous accessories were sold at military posts for $1.80. Sometimes they were used to light cigarettes, sometimes thatched huts in Vietnamese villages.

Museumgoers who look carefully at this Zippo can see a message engraved in tiny block letters on the silver casing:

WE ARE THE
    UNWILLING
LED BY THE
    UNQUALIFIED
DOING THE
    UNNECESSARY
FOR THE
    UNGRATEFUL

That's the Vietnam War, more or less, distilled into fourteen words, possibly all one really needs to know about a conflict that will take over 58,000 American and a million Vietnamese lives before it's over and, in the end, will be judged by most a terrible mistake.

But even fourteen words can be forgotten.


Just forty years later another mistake will be made as the country becomes embroiled in yet another indeterminate conflict on the other side of the world. This war will be pitched not by famous actors but by high-ranking American officials, among them the Secretary of State. He will make a speech to the United Nations, televised to the American public, replete with charts and diagrams that purport to show evidence of mobile facilities in the Mideast meant to produce weapons of mass destruction. That might lead to another mushroom cloud, a possibility that scares everyone but the skeptics, who are once again marginalized.

*I cannot tell you everything that we know. But what I can share with you, when combined with what all of us have learned over the years, is deeply troubling.*

He will be troubled again, some years after the speech, when it's clear to everyone that the WMD never existed and the ensuing invasion of Iraq by American forces was a catastrophic misjudgment. He will claim he was duped, but many will wonder if he wasn't the one doing the duping.

Some will fight for the survival of national memory itself.

At another museum in the nation's capital, in 2015, a temporary Vietnam exhibit is on view. Its study guide strives to remain relevant to contemporary students who have inherited a distrust of their own government and aren't much interested in ancient history. They need to be engaged.

*Find at least four examples in the exhibit where the U.S. government intentionally lied or misled the public through the news media.*

It's a scavenger hunt for secrets, a twenty-first-century civics lesson.

Meanwhile, new wars play in the background, a seeming constant now in American life.

An advisory is issued by the Department of Homeland Security as the conflict in the Mideast continues unabated. It concerns the new cohort of ex-military young men (and now women) in the millions who have come back from Iraq and Afghanistan. They volunteered—the draft ended in 1973—but many have seen repeated deployments. That's bound to be stressful.

*The return of military veterans facing significant challenges reintegrating into their communities could lead to the potential emergence of terrorist groups or lone wolf extremists capable of carrying out violent attacks.*

It's as if this is the first time anyone has thought about it.

By now shootings have also become part of the American landscape, each incident capturing a news cycle until supplanted, seamlessly, by the next. Reports after the fact continue to be written, some of them hundreds of pages long.

Nothing seems to change.

It's a particularly American kind of paralysis.

In a nation prone to forgetfulness the most useful formulation going forward may be a phrase, just four words, easy to remember when all the details have disappeared. It will likely as not apply to almost any conceivable contingency.

*Here we go again.*

# 4

Shooters in some form were a part of the American landscape long before the 1960s, many of them mythologized in the popular mind while alive and sometimes after death.

By the age of twenty-one gunslinger John Wesley Hardin had reportedly shot forty men, give or take, more than Billy the Kid or Jesse James. Most of them, he figured, had deserved it.

He became the most wanted man in Texas.

The Texas Rangers put out a notice in 1875 warning a possibly credulous public to be wary of beguilement: *Though courteous and well-dressed, he is extremely dangerous and always armed.*

In 1967, Bob Dylan would burnish the Hardin persona in a ballad (*he was never known / to hurt an honest man*).

Hardin had begun to shape his own legend by writing an autobiography after his capture (*The Life of John Wesley Hardin as Told By Himself*). The possibly fanciful recollections were still in print a hundred years later.

He also wrote letters from prison, studied law, and supervised the Sunday School.

Occasionally, he tried to escape, and was once reprimanded for *conspiring to incite impudence.*


From his cell he presided over family life, as if he were a farmer or a clerk who just happened to be away for a while.

*Don't be mad at ma, be mad at me*, he wrote his wife, after she confessed to ill feelings towards her in-law.

His mother worried over him (*my sweet boy*) but was resolute: *The Bible tells us they that bear the cross shall wear the crown.*

To his sons, he had but one admonition: *If any man assail your rights, your life, or your character, you have a perfect right to kill.*

Those who shunned such a duty were, in his estimation, *not worthy to be called an american.*

He served seventeen years and received a full pardon. Within a year of his release he was shot in the back by someone he'd slighted, who was himself killed by someone else a year later.

Hardin knew that a man with a gun and a grievance was always dangerous.

He had also wondered, at least once, if it was really possible to escape the past. It wasn't law enforcement that worried him.

*I was never afraid of anything except ghosts.*

# 5

A century later, the FBI will develop a system to track active shooter incidents across the country. In 2014 it issues a catalog of such occurrences spanning a thirteen-year period, along with charts. It's a methodical postmortem of each event (no one calls them accidents anymore) detailing the essentials: date, place, time of day, weapons, victims, resolution. *160 incidents, 486 killed, 557 wounded* (shooters are now officially excluded from the tallies). The incidents are color-coded according to category and constitute a mosaic of *violent acts and shootings occurring in a place of public use*. That qualification is important; it's meant to exclude garden-variety crimes, the casual murder or gang-related activity. To make this more selective roster, one has to move aggressively into the public realm, where strangers (here called *citizens*) become targets. The event may start at a residence, involving family members or an ex, but it will usually end, at random, somewhere else.

A total of 265 handguns, shotguns, and rifles are used in the 160 incidents, which suggests, if one does the math, that even the average shooter now has an arsenal.


A *Study of Active Shooter Incidents in the United States Between* 2000 *and 2013* is placed in the public domain, no permission necessary to pass it on. Its advisories are meant to reach the widest possible audience, as if information itself can serve as a shield against all those *unsubs* out there, somewhere, waiting to strike. As it happens, most such events end in minutes, long before law enforcement can arrive, so the ordinary person caught in the crosshairs can't expect help. Developing the ability to make *life or death decisions* may depend on a familiarity with past scenarios.

Discerning patterns is difficult, but a few trends are hinted at in the breakdown. Stay out of malls on Sunday, stay away from work on Wednesday if you're management, avoid campuses or streets and interstates on Fridays. Or move to one of the ten states out of fifty that were entirely free of such shootings.

It's training, of a sort, now available to everybody.


School shootings are indelibly impressed in the popular mind, but most such incidents occur in the workplace—in the offices, factories, small companies, and coffee shops spread languidly across the American landscape. Trouble may erupt in a car wash, hair salon, supermarket, or aerobics studio, or possibly in a dental office or law firm. Eating at IHOP, Burger King, or Wendy's could be chancy; shopping at Target, RadioShack, Walmart, or Best Buy might be ill-advised.

It's not just customers who are at risk. Shooting at coworkers is common, though many have no personal connection to the shooter.

Sometimes they're just other associates, caught in the wrong aisle or on the wrong shift, ready targets for a desperation that isn't reflected in labor statistics. The specific incitements seem to revolve around the stresses of trying to make a living in modern America. (Other factors, such as racial or religious animus, have been folded into the new category of *hate crimes*.) Several of the shooters, it's discovered, were fired earlier in the day, or threatened with layoffs, or passed over for promotion. A few return to the workplace months or years after losing a job. Other triggers: a reprimand from a supervisor, a change to the retirement plan, a canceled Christmas bonus. Sometimes a lawsuit has been filed, but that promises a kind of slow-motion satisfaction that may not be immediate enough. One shooter at a food processing plant waits until mid-shift to start firing. It's impossible to determine whether he's patient or impulsive.

In one Walmart incident the shooter, an employee, buys ammunition at the store just before the shooting, a transactional loop that Henry Ford would recognize. Worker and customer merged into one efficient entity: it's a classic American model shifted now to the low-wage workplace.

Of course, this particular customer-coworker won't survive to purchase anything else.

Occasionally, the incidents exhibit a seasonal aspect, as in the one where a twenty-two-year-old, hanging around a mall in Happy Valley, Oregon, shoots at people waiting to see Santa Claus. (He will kill two and wound one before committing suicide.) Sometimes, gender comes into play: almost half the women are killed by someone they're trying to get away from, a boyfriend or husband who won't let go. If the intended target isn't on-site, someone else gets shot.

Several of the incidents occur in what the FBI terms *open space*, a category that encompasses whatever occurs outside a building. One seventeen-year-old in New Jersey starts shooting as he wanders through a carnival crowd. That's anomalous; the other such events play out on the open road, with young or middle-aged males firing from a moving vehicle. These encounters last longer than most; collectively, they blur into one another, the same action sequence played over and over. Across Oklahoma, Pennsylvania, New Mexico, Texas, Alabama, Florida, Washington, they're all on the run until the road runs out. Usually, that means a showdown with police. In one instance, the lethal joyride is cut short at a gas pump.

One graphic in the report crisply conveys a phenomenon that the FBI takes care to underscore, as if it were surprising: all but six of the 160 shooters are male. *Cathline, Amy, Jennifer, Latina, Arunya, Yvonne*—obviously gendered names—are followed by the designation *(female)* as the relevant incidents are recorded. It seems a cryptic commentary. But no further explanation is forthcoming, so readers are left to tease out insights on their own.

Some gender differences are discernible. Unlike the male shooters, the women carry just one weapon, always a handgun. Most are in their forties. None shoots a domestic partner. Just two of the six commit suicide; the others surrender, sometimes after being overpowered.

All told, they kill fifteen people and wound seven.

Possible inferences: It seems natural for men to commit such crimes, but unnerving when women act accordingly. Or women start later in life and travel more lightly than men.

Or women can feel as abused or disturbed as men, but are far less likely to act on it, particularly in public, so these six are outliers and nothing to worry about; alternatively, they display a kind of self-assertion that usually only males exhibit, so even a small uptick in the numbers going forward may indicate a troublesome trend.

Or, simpler still: women aren't any happier working in a maintenance yard, supermarket, factory, post office, or university than anyone else, but no one likes to lose even a lousy job, in which case these actions, while aberrant, fall within a recognizable range of responses.

As to why women don't pursue domestic partners, like their enraged male counterparts, it may be that some men can't stand to be alone, while women are more resilient. Or women aren't constitutionally predisposed to violence, even if provoked; alternatively, relentless socialization may have encouraged a kind of learned helplessness, so that while every fifteen minutes, on average, an American woman is beaten in her own home (contextual information that isn't reflected in this account), she may simply resign herself to a bad relationship, especially if she's broke or raising a child.

But ruminations on the national psyche fall outside the scope of the FBI report.

Anyway, no one's much interested in the *why* any longer. Studies like this are more a reflexive nod to due diligence, something to undertake while waiting for the next seemingly inevitable event.

It's a matter now of adjusting to a new reality in American life, getting used to the notion that once benign phrases like *open season* or *spree* have been repurposed, and the guy (or gal) next door probably has a gun.

As a popular 1980s cop show once cautioned, *be careful out there.*

Meanwhile, material continues to accumulate for the next FBI report.

Over the five-year period from 2014 to 2019, almost two thousand mass shootings are logged in the United States by those monitoring the mayhem.

Some incidents stand out from the general blur.

On October 1, 2017, a sixty-four-year-old gunman, acting alone, fires from the thirty-second floor of a hotel into a crowd of 22,000 people attending an outdoor music event in Las Vegas. He kills fifty-nine and wounds over five hundred before killing himself.

It becomes the deadliest mass shooting to date in modern American history, and the first since the Whitman incident in which a shooter fires from high above his targets.

In the immediate aftermath of the event neighbors and family are bewildered; the shooter's brother, anguished, can only sputter. *It's like an asteroid hit. He had a girlfriend.*

In other words, it's inexplicable.

But a more specific advisory is now available to anxious citizens: *be careful at concerts.*

# 6

Business opportunities abound for those nimble enough to identify niche markets and adapt to new needs. If workplace violence is a given, there's money to be made in recognizing that reality. *Americans spend half their waking hours inside the buildings where they work*, one such company advertises, and no one is safe (the FBI survey has definitively established that unfortunate fact). But start-ups like ShotSpotter and Shooter Detection Systems have developed the technology to give proactive companies an edge.

Better to know exactly what you're up against.

State-of-the-art sensors can instantly detect *sharp acoustic events* in any properly equipped area; additionally, infrared cameras detect flashes, so gunfire can be confirmed the moment it occurs (no more relying on the guesswork of panicked employees). Precision instruments report the data: *number of rounds fired, location of shooters inside building,*

It's even possible to provide streaming audio files of each event.

These new systems can be integrated into existing security set-ups, so they're cost-effective.

For businesses that choose not to invest in more comprehensive packages, there are other options, such as the 30-minute *Online Active-Shooter Preparedness Training Course.* It's an abbreviated sequence that focuses on ways in which management can mitigate the impact of such events. With guidance, staff can be encouraged to think clearly under stress, the kind of stress that ensues when you're not sure what's going on and haven't counted the shots or figured out who's where, and you're worried about survival.

The ability to implement one of the classic emergency options—*Leave, Hide, or Act*—is critical to a bystander's well-being. Technology is no substitute for timely actions undertaken after training.

And an online course is both cost-effective and convenient.

The need for ancillary services doesn't end with the event itself. Often, in the aftermath, specialists in *biohazard remediation* (more commonly known as crime scene cleanup) have to be called in. It's a more complicated process than one would think, given the propensity of blood-borne pathogens to cling to rugs, floors, walls, and stray surfaces. Bacteria and biological material can't be eliminated with ordinary cleaning agents. Expertise is necessary. A familiarity with best practices is advisable. Most people, whether at home or at the office, wouldn't know where to start.

Fortunately, professionals in the private sector are available to assist.

*Bio is all we do,* an industry leader advertises. Their trauma cleaning teams are positioned throughout the nation, outside *major metros,* ready to respond within hours to any site in the continental United States (it's effectively an after-the-fact SWAT operation). All major credit cards are accepted. A wide range of clients, in civilian life and law enforcement, call on the company. The initial cleanup phase (including surface testing) scrubs and sanitizes, but the more encompassing goal is to restore a space to its pre-trauma condition, all traces erased of the crime, suicide, accident, or mass shooting. It's a way to reverse engineer catastrophe so that routines can be resumed, property values restored, lives rebuilt.

Scars may remain, but they won't be visible.

# 7

One such site the company cleans up is a well-appointed suburban home in Connecticut with *pale yellow wooden siding and green shutters*, according to the state police report. The team doesn't have much to do. Aside from the master bedroom, where the event occurred, most of the house looks like it's never been lived in, the crime scene photos documenting almost impossibly uncluttered spaces. The walls are painted in soothing off whites. There's a copy of *Delicious Living* on the kitchen table. Counters and floors gleam; paper towels in the wastebasket have been carefully folded alongside a neatly cut apple core. The interiors of the fridge and bathroom vanity are immaculate. In the office, cookbooks and travel guides stand resolutely upright beside Red Sox memorabilia, the book spines providing rare slashes of color in an otherwise carefully muted setting.

There is one clearly incongruous element—a bedroom with windows masked by black plastic garbage bags. But the bed's been neatly made.

The police report describes the house as *well-maintained above average*, which seems an understatement. Someone has almost willed this order into being.

That person would probably be the fifty-two-year-old female lying in bed upstairs with *four projectiles* in her head. She was killed, according to official conjectures, by *other relative residing in house*. That would almost certainly be her twenty-year-old son, Adam Lanza, using the Savage Mark II .22 caliber bolt-action rifle, serial number 1605038, that she had purchased the year before. He would go on to kill 27 others at Sandy Hook Elementary School—including children, teachers, and finally himself—on that day of December 14, 2012, in the worst mass shooting since Virginia Tech some five years earlier.

But Nancy Lanza would be his first victim. It will never be clear whether her murder was prompted by malice or mercy.

None of the several neighbors interviewed in days following had noticed anything unusual, or suspicious, in the vicinity of the house on Yogananda Street that week. It had always been a quiet neighborhood. Most of them wouldn't have recognized the Lanza family, though at least one knew that the woman was divorced and raising a difficult child by herself. They probably weren't aware that he had an older brother in another state, or a father who hadn't seen his youngest son in two years, though he made fitful attempts at connection.

They certainly couldn't know that the events of that day would constitute a kind of endgame for mother and son, a tangled relationship resolved in a single explosive morning.

One of the neighbors remembered hearing shots at about 9 a.m., *probably* a *hunter*. No one thought twice about the oil truck outside the house at 9:30, or its driver, who hadn't himself seen anyone on the premises in at least five years. He'd always been instructed to leave the bills in the mailbox. Someone had always paid them.

By 11:30, however, something unusual was undeniably unfolding in the area.

If neighbors hadn't noticed the sniper team fanning outward on the Lanza property, establishing a *perimeter*, they would almost certainly have seen the RG-12 Armored Vehicle inching up the driveway as now-established protocols were put into place. At this point police themselves knew little, except the address the shooter had left in his car. A second shooter might be waiting inside; the premises might be booby-trapped; the two packages the UPS driver attempted to deliver might be IEDs. (The boxes were opened on-site, gingerly, and determined to be *personal products for the residence*.) One couldn't be too cautious; everything now had to be considered suspicious.

Most important protocol: one step at a time.


First the residence has to be secured, doors breached by one team and rooms cleared by another. It takes police twenty minutes to reach the second floor, where they find the body. There are protocols for this kind of discovery as well. *The female did not respond to verbal direction.* They observe a BLS (*blood-like substance*) on the bedding, though that will have to be confirmed by the lab. A rifle rests on the floor.

By this time Nancy Lanza had been dead for almost three hours, which will be established, officially, by the paramedic on the scene.

Calls to the answering machine are meticulously logged. Expanding reaction to the event can be tracked in the twenty-some phone messages to the house that begin at 11:48 a.m. The first call comes from state police, who do not receive an answer (noted in the reports as *negative contact*). Over the next several hours calls begin to accumulate from media venues: local outlets, and the nationals—CBS, CNN, ABC, *The Huffington Post*, Headline News, the Dr. Phil show.

Everyone wants more information, including the family itself.

At 1:50 p.m. Ryan Lanza, in Hoboken, leaves a message *asking his mom to call him*. An hour later, his grandmother calls: *Nancy, this is mom . . .*

Throughout the day messages from unidentified individuals come in, constituting a kind of impromptu choral response from the community. In midafternoon a female voice sends condolences to the family. In counterpoint, a series of male voices offer other thoughts: *Your son's a pussy . . . Shitty ass parents . . . Is this the motherfucker who killed those kids?* At 10:30 p.m., in the last call of the day, another male voice: *Your son deserves to be dead.*

The messages echo, undelivered, in a now empty house.


The shootings at Sandy Hook were over in just eight minutes; the investigative work to follow would take almost two years. The Lanza family had been left to its own devices, more or less, for a very long time, but now their lives would be subject to exhaustive scrutiny. In 1966, the investigation of the Charles Whitman shooting had concluded with an expert report of twenty-some pages; forty-six years later, the Sandy Hook shootings would result in official reports totaling several hundred pages.

In neither case would any finding be declared definitive.

The Sandy Hook investigation begins the day of the shooting. Items of *evidentiary value* are inventoried and removed from the Lanza home for analysis. They include a cache of sixteen blank day planners and a To Do list extending through December 20, *authored by Nancy Lanza*, along with a box of her children's artwork.

So far, a typical parent, perhaps more organized than most.

Of greater interest to investigators are the guns kept in the house:

the Savage rifle, an Enfield .323 bolt-action rifle, a Bushmaster XM15 rifle, Saiga 12-gauge semiautomatic shotgun, AR-15 automatic rifle, Glock 20 10mm handgun, and a Sig Sauer P226 9mm pistol. One gun isn't in the group—the Smith & Wesson .38 snub nose revolver a friend had recommended she buy for personal protection after she had asked for advice. If she did the research, she would have discovered that the *Snubby* was often promoted by gun shops for first-time buyers and for women, but many enthusiasts felt a larger gun might be more effective, something like a Glock, which your average woman could master more easily.

Police also discover over a thousand rounds of ammunition in the house, some of it in ziplock bags, along with the paraphernalia associated with diligent gun stewardship: cleaning kits, instruction manuals, a gun safe for storage. Everything's legal: the paperwork has been collected in a blue folder neatly labeled *Guns*.

They will later learn that Nancy Lanza had grown up with guns, liked hunting, and had often gone target shooting with her husband and sons. That was something Adam had always enjoyed, and both parents felt it was a way to spend time with him. She believed in responsible gun ownership; both she and Adam had taken an NRA gun safety course. And, a friend remembered, she was *very proud of her firearm collection.*

Investigators also discover the holiday gift she had already prepared for her son, a check to be presented on Christmas Day for the purchase of a CZ 83 semi-automatic pistol—military surplus, highly rated by those who seek a reliable weapon under $300.

That gun would not be added to the collection.


Nancy Lanza had once said she wasn't afraid of Adam, she was afraid *for* him: afraid, presumably, of what the world would do to

the needy, troubled child when she wasn't around anymore to protect him. An Asperger's syndrome/OCD diagnosis was, at bottom,
just a crude catchall for the thousand maddening perplexities of everyday life that had to be negotiated from the moment he woke up
each day: accommodations to the three-year-old who couldn't stand
to be touched, who flinched at noise, who spoke a fantasy language
only she could translate; to the boy who wouldn't accept expressions
of affection, disliked holidays, and didn't want a Christmas tree; to
the teenager who developed exacting food rituals, didn't want her
to lean on counters or tables, and was disturbed by the slightest
disruption in routine. He was terrified when Hurricane Sandy hit,
but wouldn't leave the house for a hotel though they lost power for
three days. She wouldn't leave without him. She decided afterwards
to buy a generator in preparation for the next storm.

There was always something else to put on the To-Do list.

Over the years she had occasionally observed, cautiously, that he
was getting better, *but . . .* There was always a *but*. One couldn't expect a cure, just stability, and, possibly, college, a job, maybe something more. In the meantime, what investigators would later term
her hypervigilant management of his symptoms had become a way
of life, by her own admission *a high-stress, 24/7 operation.*


She was bright but left college after three years when she married.
It was a decision she later regretted. She left the workplace to raise
the two boys when they came, volunteering at women's shelters and
schools as time allowed. She was known to be generous to family
and friends. Sometimes she expressed frustration that her workaholic husband paid less attention than she did to the family, but he
was around on weekends and there were, she confided to a friend,
*worse things than being a workaholic.*

There were always worse things.

For a time she thought she had developed a serious illness, something like MS, or some other neurological disorder that might be terminal. She told friends that doctors had *poked, prodded, tortured* her but couldn't nail a diagnosis down. She resolved to stay positive, *not dwell on the negative*, and kept her worries from the family. By this time she had divorced, and her ex had remarried. They remained on amicable terms.

Investigators would later find no medical evidence of any disorder, intimating that her possibly imagined health concerns, *a fixation with her health and mortality*, may have diverted attention from the needs of her son. It would have been better, perhaps, had she suppressed her own anxieties.

That's what wives and mothers were supposed to do.


The family cycled through a series of educational settings for Adam as he grew older. Sometimes, a new situation would seem to be working but, inevitably, issues would arise. The school would alert her; she would acknowledge their concern, thank them, promise a solution: *I will get on it first thing in the morning. I will think of something.*

The record reflects a blizzard of communications sent, regularly, to various school officials and a series of psychologists. She was sometimes dispirited; some of the psych evaluations did not seem to contain *even a glimmer of hope.*

She needed hope.

Eventually, she decided that her son would do better at home, with a tutor, or taking a class at the local community college. Even then, it was touch and go. At one point he had what she described as a meltdown, began to cry and couldn't stop. She sent an anxious e-mail to her ex-husband: *I don't know what I should do.*

He didn't know either.

In later years it wasn't just her son who had withdrawn; she had withdrawn with him, into the house, tentatively tethered to the outside world by texts and e-mails. During one period the two communicated with each other, at his insistence, only by computer. Their exchanges were surprisingly expansive, as if it were easier to talk through an intermediary.

> *I type nothing in this that is in a tone that is condescending, vindictive, malicious, snide, malignant, or any synonym that you can think of. I mean well. If you believe that you wasted your life, as you seem to have insinuated, you will gain nothing from regretting it . . . What you should do is think about what you want to do . . . I do not try to avoid doing anything for you as you seem to think. I am glad that I was born, and I appreciate your having taken care of me.*

> . . .

> *I appreciate your effort to be a comfort to me. I apologize if I seemed angry or antagonistic. I was simply over emotional and as it is often the case worrying about the future . . . in no way do I regret having raised two wonderful children. I have high hopes for you both and will consider my life a success if you and Ryan live happy and productive lives . . . I am much happier now, knowing that you do not despise me for bringing you into this world.*

Friends and acquaintances offered conflicting perspectives on their relationship, as observed from afar; one thought he had no emotional connection to his mother, a sentiment she sometimes shared; another thought they were close; another, *Adam never appreciated what Nancy did for him.*

No perspective could be considered conclusive.

The official reports will note, in a chastening subtext, that Nancy Lanza had created a *prosthetic* environment for her son, essentially molding the world around him to his moods. Like many such parents, she was, they declared, essentially in denial. He needed more than she could possibly provide. They acknowledged that various well-intentioned professionals had done little to help her along the way. In any event, police would conclude, *The investigation has not discovered any evidence that Nancy Lanza was in any way aware of her son's plans.*

One wonders what she might have thought about such assessments.

How could outsiders, strangers, people who referred to her son as *A.L.* and apologized to readers for describing him *in what appear to be human terms,* ever imagine what she felt, her duty to the damaged child she loved and may sometimes have wished had never been born? How could her *years of service and sacrifice,* as she once put it, mean so little?

That's another question that will never be answered.

On December 11, Nancy Lanza traveled by herself to New Hampshire. The three-day trip was intended as a trial to see how Adam fared on his own at home, in preparation for what she hoped might be a new start for them somewhere else. It was also, possibly, a respite for her: a return to the state in which she'd grown up, dreamed, imagined a life, before her world contracted so precipitously to the stark property on Yogananda Street.

She checked into a hotel and shopped at outlet stores. She caught up with a high school friend she hadn't seen since the 1970s. Official records indicate she had a nice dinner alone on the first night, eating mussels, crab cakes, chard, and bread pudding with wine. She had a salmon salad, more chard, chocolate mousse, and more wine on the following evening, and ordered a $4 muffin from room service ($5.86 with tax and tip) the next day. And then the trip was over.

She got home at 10p.m. the night before the shootings.

The book she was reading at her death was found by police on the floor beside her bed, half-finished, with several passages marked by Post-its. *Train Your Brain to Get Happy: The Simple Program That Primes Your Grey Cells for Joy, Optimism, and Serenity.* It contains some trendy exhortations (*turn that frown upside down*) along with slightly more nuanced notes on cognitive behavioral therapies and meditation techniques. It is the kind of book that might appeal to someone who felt, given the time and the resolve, that anything was still possible.

And, if all else were to fail, there was another suggestion: *Forgive yourself.*

The house on Yogananda Street was still vacant two years after the shootings. Neighbors and townspeople found it difficult to pass by the property, with its reminders of what some termed *the evil that resided there.* In January 2015 the Newtown Legislative Council voted to demolish the structure, leaving open space in its stead, in hopes that the haunted community might begin to move on.

# 8

On March 24, 2018, over a million people marched in localities across the nation to demand that someone do something about guns in American life. The event was led by student survivors of the February 2018 shooting that would thereafter be known as *Parkland*—one high school, one shooter, one semiautomatic rifle, seventeen victims, fresh outrage, a new generation galvanized and angry. The brother of a Sandy Hook victim was among them.

It was the largest student mobilization since the Vietnam protests of the 1960s.

In the moment it seemed that the proverbial tipping point had been reached, that students declaring *we will change the world* might actually do so. They were supported by a wide swath of citizens, celebrities, corporate entities, and religious leaders. Surely such energy—focused, insistent, unapologetic—would move the needle, now.

But others weren't so sure. They had been there before. *It's just too soon to tell.*

In 2019, after another series of mass shootings, and additional outrage, cracks began to form in a corporate culture that had long championed gun rights. Walmart, the world's largest retailer, decreed it would no longer sell the ammo needed for assault rifles, though it would continue to service shotgun owners and sport shooters. A major grocery store chain ended its open carry gun policy. Colt, producer of pistols, revolvers, and rifles for nearly two hundred years (among them John Wesley Hardin's favorite firearm) announced it would no longer sell AR-15s for the civilian market. Consumers would have to rely upon the dozens of other companies that manufactured the weapon.

Some in the public relations community hailed the shift: *This is a major move.*

But the companies themselves were careful to assure the public that certain long-held principles were still sacrosanct in the American marketplace.

*Colt has been a stout supporter of the Second Amendment for over 180 years, remains so, and will continue to provide its customers with the finest quality firearms in the world.*

*Soldiers*

*Over forty million Americans have served since the country's inception in what is now the world's third largest military.*

*Sometimes we learn their names, like Nelson, Noreen, Ellis, Bolty, Laughton, Rossi, Manning. Sometimes we learn their stories. But for the most part the individual elements of this vast machinery seem to be interchangeable, from a distance, like one great weapon that is continually reconstituted.*

*'Thank you for your service' has become a reflexive salutation directed by civilians to anyone who wears a uniform. In a nation with a volunteer army, it's the new way of doing one's part.*

*The military ethos permeates our everyday language; those who would never themselves deploy still live to fight another day or choose the hill they want to die on, as the saying goes, in the office or at home.*

*And 'gung ho' no longer means 'work together,' as the original*

*Chinese expression had it, but is now an American idiom suggesting a feeling bordering on belligerence.*

*Such casual habituation to conflict has helped to create a vicarious warrior culture in which most of us just watch from afar.*

*It wasn't always that way.*

# I

*Made Electrician's Mate 3rd Class. Also, V-J day.*
—Jimmy's war diary, Sept. 2, 1945

His name was Jimmy; no one ever called him James. Lincoln High School, Seattle, Washington, class of 1944, grandchild of immigrants from Scandinavia. He had never traveled anywhere in his eighteen years; he had not yet drunk a beer or done much of anything with a woman.

He could have been any one of thousands of eighteen-year-olds drafted in August 1944, called from all over the country to follow their older brothers into battle. A few of them became Jimmy's buddies, guys like *Noreen, Ellis, Bolty, Laughton, Rossi*. Their company would remind him of high school, in a good way.

His father had said *stay out of the army*, and Jimmy had listened, opting to play the odds in the navy instead. The Oath of

Allegiance he was handed upon induction was prefaced by extra material that he was expected to ponder. It was like a school assignment, only serious.

*Like most of the men who have come here to enlist, you have probably never thought that you owe anything to your country.*

No argument there.

*Probably, this is the first time you have ever taken an oath. Do you know what an oath is? An oath is a solemn promise.*

He could make a promise.

*You must have for your country a feeling like that which a man has for a good mother.*

That must be a metaphor, or maybe a simile, he could never keep them straight.

*The government must come before even your family.*

That was a harder sell. His father was family, but also the smartest man he'd ever met, someone the government ought to listen to itself.

He took the oath, with that reservation.

He didn't reflect on the power of the State to put his life on hold, much less resist it. He didn't wonder about larger questions or abstractions. That wasn't the kind of discussion he or his friends engaged in. Anyway, everybody knew it was a good war. And the navy had covered its bases.

*After you take the oath, your motto should be: "My country—may she ever be right! But, right or wrong, my country!"*

By the time he got to the war, things in Europe were winding down and the brass were making plans to invade Japan. They would need a force of several million men to pull it off.

Jimmy, waiting in the Philippines, was pretty sure he'd be one of them.

If he had watched *Why We Fight*, the government-sanctioned film shown to most incoming servicemen, he would have learned about the *Yamato spirit* of the Japanese people, their ancient willingness to sacrifice and die, if necessary, for emperor or nation. *Each living Japanese is merely a link in this endless chain of ghosts.* It was enough to give an American kid the willies, this exotic notion that he was up against something he couldn't even see. He had already heard about *Jap treachery, sneak punches, Pearl,* and he was scared.

But he would never say anything like that out loud.

Abruptly, a year to the day after his induction, out of the blue, a surprise weapon called an *A-bomb* is dropped, and that's it. *Base wild. Nobody goes to bed. Ships light harbor, band out, free beer.*

Jimmy would be going to Japan after all, but as part of an occupation. From then on, as he would later put it, *the war was fun.*

—

She would be over ninety years old now, the young Japanese woman whose picture is pasted into his scrapbook, above the caption *My*

*little Jap girlfriend in Yokosuka,* alongside the two stamps she gave him for the letter she hoped he would write. The man posing stiffly on the stamps is Admiral Tōgō Heihachirō, 1848–1934, revered naval strategist, mentor to Emperor Hirohito himself. Jimmy would probably not have cared about all that. He did take pains to spell out the girl's name phonetically—*Soo/ge/u/la Ma/sa/ka*—and one imagines him practicing the pronunciation, chopping up the syllables in his clumsy American accent, trying to remember which name would come first in English.

They probably laughed about it.

In the snapshot she stands, smiling, in front of an elegant home. But the girl in the picture is already gone, along with the life she had lived in a fragile city made of paper and wood. *Picture taken at her house in Tokyo, which was destroyed by B-29 raid.* That might have been the raid in March 1944 that consumed sixteen square miles of the city, killing 100,000 in a ravenous firestorm fed by napalm and white phosphorus.

The night sky was lit up for hours.

It took hundreds of B-29s to do that damage, wave after wave scattering incendiaries onto the ground below; later, survivors of the A-bomb attacks in Hiroshima and Nagasaki would note that no one had considered the single B-29 flying above them anything to worry about.

Thirty percent of the people of Tokyo on that March night were suddenly homeless.

By that time Japan was desperately short of almost everything— steel, concrete, fuel—and adequate homes and shelters could no longer be built. People were sleeping on the streets. If planes came, they were told to dig holes in the ground and cover themselves with dirt. There wasn't much food, or much of anything else, except devastation.

No wonder a girl might harbor a secret hope that this sweet American sailor would take her away from the ruin around her.

But Jimmy only spent a week in Yokosuka. He never wrote that letter, and *Soo/ge/u/la* never lived that imagined life.

His scrapbook is full of service mementos cataloged with care, as if he were on special duty as an archivist—chits for ice cream, beer, and cigarettes, USO tickets, military transport checks, a spreadsheet listing letters sent and received, sick bay slips (*Complaint: Sickness*), medical clearance slips (*free from vermin and communicable diseases*), menus of special meals, newspaper clips from home that his mother faithfully sent (*"Half of Sailor's Navy Life is Spent Standing in Lines"*).

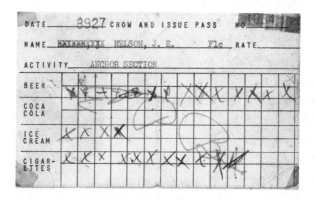

She sent news of other Lincoln High classmates when she could, and each of the articles went into the scrapbook. John, a flyer, had gone missing over Germany in April 45, one mission shy of his twenty-fifth and final flight; Bert was wounded in action somewhere else; Arvid, 4F, ran the library bookmobile in Seattle; Violet Rose, at home, married a navy man named Marvin who had survived Pearl Harbor, Iwo Jima,

and Okinawa before his discharge. That got him a front-row seat to
the Japanese surrender on the USS *Missouri* in Tokyo Bay.

In a section of his scrapbook titled "Naval Vocabulary" he de-
voted several pages to the unfamiliar terminology he was encoun-
tering in the service. It was like studying another language. A *mate*
might be *on the ball, pie-eyed, full of bull,* a *sack rat,* a *muff diver,*
or *a barnacle* (someone you can't lose). A female might be *stacked,*
a *business woman* (native whore), or *state-side stuff* (white woman).
A sailor with a wife was *dragging anchor.* An officer was a *90-day
wonder*; medics were *pecker checkers. Chaplain's duty* meant con-
soling a crybaby. Depending on circumstances, a guy might *drift
around, hit the deck, haul ass,* or *chew the fat.*

He learned how to say *good morning, hurry up, dick,* and *friend*
in Filipino.

He documented his tour on the USS *Pratt Victory,* a minesweeper
manned by volunteers known as the Guinea Pig Squadron. As a late
draftee, single and childless, Jimmy would be one of the last to be
decommissioned, but if he sought out hazardous duty he'd jump the
line by earning extra points. American forces had planted powerful
mines throughout the Japanese waterways and harbors during the
war; now someone needed to go back and blow them up. Never one
to *drift around,* Jimmy joined up with a few others who were aiming
to get some *egg in your beer* to get back to *Uncle Sugar* sooner. Their
exploits rated a 1946 article in *Newsweek: The risky job will continue until lanes used by American ships have all been swept clean.*

None of the guinea pigs wanted to go back to the States in a
*meat wagon,* but they figured the odds were on their side.

Jimmy also took lots of pictures. They were usually out of focus,
often taken after the fact, a compilation of places and experiences

that had already disappeared. He had missed the main event, but he wanted to capture what he could of whatever was left.

He travels to Okinawa, almost a tourist, taking pictures of bare ground (*this is where heaviest fighting was—no sign of a tree or bldg—must have been rough*).

He goes to the ancient city of Kobe and takes more shots of blackened earth (*city leveled by U.S. bombers—this used to be a park*).

He takes pictures of the emperor's palace in Tokyo, from a distance, getting a bit of the moat surrounding the hidden space and a few civilians scattered in the public square (*Japs on way to kneel and pray in front of Imperial Palace*).

He snaps a shot from a landing craft about to anchor in Pearl Harbor (construction cranes can be seen in the background).

He waits outside General MacArthur's Tokyo headquarters and gets a close-up shot from thirty feet away, MacArthur snapping a salute straight at him (*he's saluting guard—not me*). He doesn't mention that the man walking briskly beside MacArthur, stride for stride, is General Eisenhower, a future president; he pays attention only to his boss, *old "Mac" himself.*

Besides the big shots, there are also pictures of his buddies. Three sit jauntily on a jeep, one holding a small makeshift Christmas tree under the towering palms; hundreds of sailors are planted in a chow line that never seems to move (*food horrible—bread full of wheat bugs*), only the ones closest to the camera attempting a forlorn smile; Jimmy himself in his skivvies, wringing his wash out over a bucket (*no automatic laundromats here!*).

They all seem impossibly young, boys more than men, hardly aware that this wartime experience will mark them for the rest of their lives.

In one of the last pictures in the scrapbook Jimmy is back in Seattle, just after discharge, still in uniform. He holds up the Blue Star flag his mother had hung in the window while he was gone, the universal signal that she had a boy in the service. His caption is unsentimental, the kind of thing a toughened twenty-year-old would write, minimizing the miracle of getting back in one piece before the blue star could turn to gold.

*Take down the flag, mother—your son's home.*

The A-bomb was the closest-kept secret of the war, involving secret production sites, secret cities, the secrets of nature itself. Vice President Truman was famously kept in the dark until the urgent briefing he received after President Roosevelt suddenly died. *It seems to be the most terrible thing ever discovered,* he would write in his diary that day, leaving the more technical aspects to the experts.

Jimmy and his shipmates were informed about the bomb in the days following the detonation, in mimeographed newsletters that attempted to explain the science. *Uranium, essential to the atomic bomb, does not exist in pure form in nature.* The process of development had apparently been touch and go. *Early in 1940, the task of isolating even an infinitesimal drop of the substance appeared hopeless.* Heat, blast, and radiation are all forms of energy (something inside atoms). On paper, energy can kill.

It had been entirely theoretical until it was tested once in the desert and then deployed. It could easily have been a dud.

The secret of production of atomic bombs was kept hidden until yesterday after the first atomic bomb fell on Japan.

They learned about the effects of the blast. First comes the fireball, then the shock wave, then the mushroom cloud, and finally the fallout. The flash will last only a fraction of a second, but anyone up to a mile away will be burned; anyone looking directly at the explosion may be blinded. Temperatures in the boiling fireball will reach millions of degrees, hotter than the surface of the sun; most buildings will be obliterated in the 900-mph shock wave, and windows will be blown out five miles away. Those persons closest to the point of impact will likely be vaporized. Anyone who survives the immediate danger will need to worry about *radiation*, a killer borne by invisible particles sprayed outward from the cloud.

It would all take some getting used to.

The American public learned that the United States and Germany had both been racing to develop the weapon. It wasn't farfetched to imagine frightening counterfactuals—what might have happened to London, for instance, if an Allied city had been targeted instead, or some unsuspecting community in the Midwest. Jimmy's mother sent him an aerial view of downtown Seattle, a newspaper picture with 4.1 square miles marked off, corresponding exactly to the devastated area of Hiroshima. The headline said it all: *If Atom Bomb Hit Seattle . . .*

Better to be on the side that set off the world's most horrific weapon first.

Jimmy and his family, like many other Americans, would never question that elemental belief.


For a time, into the early 1960s, *the bomb* insinuated itself into every dark corner of American life. Parents were instructed in the most up-to-date ways to protect their families in future conflicts. The woman of the household would need to think about ordinary tasks in a new light (*After a conventional bombing laundry is generally full of glass splinters and grime; in case of atomic bombing it might be contaminated with radioactive materials*). The man of the house would be wise to build a fallout shelter (*All that is needed is a basement, some basic woodworking skills and approximately $165*). Various materials could be used in a pinch as shielding to absorb stray radiation—sixteen inches of books provided the same effective protection as twelve inches of earth, or eight inches of concrete. Food and water would need to be stockpiled. Tranquilizers were strongly suggested (*A bottle of 100 should be sufficient for a family of four*) along with a Bible and a deck of cards.

Information was the most potent weapon a citizen could possess.

President Eisenhower drafted the entire family into the effort (*Every woman and every child has practically the same duties as does any man*). He urged Congress to fund an interstate highway system that would ensure rapid evacuation of major cities. Children

learned to dive under desks; friendly cartoon figures showed them
how to duck and cover if they were outdoors.

President Kennedy directed the Army Corps of Engineers to design a fallout shelter for his own home at Hyannis Port.

In Operation Alert, a nationwide simulation of a nuclear attack,
elaborate drills were conducted over several years in sixty American
cities. In one especially grim scenario fatalities were estimated at
eight million, with twelve million injured; fallout spread over 63,000
square miles. National newspapers dutifully reported the make-
believe devastation the next day. In New York, *203,000 killed as
A-bomb hits Bronx*; in Buffalo, *125,000 known dead, Downtown
in Ruins*; on the west coast, *One Million 'Casualties' in California.*

All in preparation for the fateful announcement that could come
at any moment: *This is not a test.*

Over time, inevitably, the fear of nuclear holocaust receded with the
decline of the Cold War. Maybe it wasn't such a big deal after all.
Some of the later atomic literature consciously backed away from
the dramatic and became more matter-of-fact.

*Atom splitting is just another way of causing an explosion.* But the scientists who understood the bomb best were never cavalier about its power. They believed the public was sleepwalking into annihilation, more likely than not, sooner or later, after the shelters had fallen into disrepair and people forgot how frightened they had once been. Technology was developing that made Hiroshima seem primitive. Someday, a bomb could conceivably be packed into a suitcase. And there was a lot of unsecured nuclear material floating around. The Bulletin of Atomic Scientists sounded the alarm, every few years, lamenting public disregard of the danger. Its founders had established the Doomsday Clock, a simple mechanism to make the peril as visceral as possible. It was a countdown to global cataclysm, with midnight representing the end of the world.

In 1947, the first clock was set at seven minutes to midnight.

Over the next several decades the clock jumped back and forth as world events warranted, sometimes set to two minutes to midnight (the United States and Russia both develop an H-bomb), sometimes seventeen (bilateral cuts in nuclear arsenals). It was rarely over nine.

In 2015 the clock was set to three minutes to midnight: *The probability of global catastrophe is very high.*

But only a few people still paid attention to Armageddon by that point. Most had other problems.

Can't make a mortgage payment: *5 minutes to midnight.* Partner walks out: *4 minutes to midnight.* Cop approaching: *3 minutes to midnight.* Lose a job: *2 minutes to midnight.* Strange spot on X-ray: *1 minute to midnight.*

There were thousands of alarms in daily life, always going off, deafening to those in trouble, undetected by anyone else. It was always just minutes to midnight for somebody.

*E pluribus unum: out of many, one*—an aspiration, rarely a reality. Except in moments of national crisis, Americans had usually been on their own. The twentieth century just gave them a new word for it: *atomized*.

—

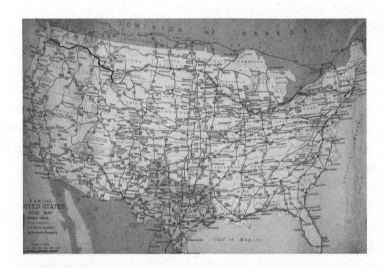

After the war Jimmy and a buddy drove for two months around the United States.

He kept a meticulous record of the trip (*10,802 miles, 32 states, 11 flat tires, $230 cost*) and marked the map as they inched across it. Most nights they slept in the car or on cots under the open sky.

He'd seen the world; now he wanted to see his own country.

He had mixed feelings about Minneapolis (*poor crop of women*).

He was impressed by Niagara Falls (*really spectacular*).

He had never seen anything like October in New England (*hills covered with beautiful leaves*).

He went out of his way to visit Lexington and Concord, where the first shot of the Revolution was fired, but it was a letdown, just empty ground (*couldn't find anything historic*).

In New York City he bought socks at Macy's and commented on the traffic (*all drive like crazy men*).

He toured the White House in Washington, D.C., hiked to the top of the Washington Monument, looked up at the Lincoln Memorial, and spent a few hours in the Smithsonian.

Sometimes it was *hot as the devil*, other times *cold as ice*.

They ran afoul of the law in Vero, Florida (*cop stopped us after someone reported we were suspicious looking*).

He got a haircut in Tampa and bought two dozen oranges for fifteen cents.

In Key West, he took President Truman's picture.

He was disappointed in the Alamo (*not a fort, just a mission*), liked the Grand Canyon, loved Yosemite.

All told, he judged the trip a resounding success: *saw everything*.

He shook hands with the buddy he had spent two months with, wished him well, and never saw or spoke to him again.


Jimmy Nelson later married and became a successful corporate attorney. He traveled the world many times over but was always happiest coming home to Seattle. He never questioned his postwar prosperity; he just enjoyed it. Late in life, in a rare moment of regret, he wondered why he hadn't done more for other people, those strangers who always seemed to need help. Then he remembered the war years and, for a time, felt better.

He passed away on the Fourth of July, which probably would have pleased him.

He was survived by his wife and the children of his widowed sister, kids he had always treated like his own when he thought himself childless.

Had he lived a few years longer he might have learned, thanks to Ancestry.com, that he had possibly fathered twin daughters he never knew about, infants put up for adoption in a distant city by a single professional woman in the 1960s. She probably valued her privacy and hoped her secret would be kept forever.

But few secrets would be safe in a world in thrall to powerful new capabilities.

# 2

The woman in the crosshairs is wearing a hijab, a child walking down the street at her side. She can't see the Apache helicopter as it hovers above her, more than a mile away, but it can see her, its camera drifting in lazy circles over her neighborhood as it zooms in and out. It might be her laundry that's strung across a nearby terrace, or someone she knows who's now lying motionless on the curb as she passes. Or maybe that's just a mound of garbage, hard to tell from the fuzzy black-and-white footage.

The $14 million Apache, code-named *Crazyhorse*, is state of the art, armed with Hellfire missiles and 30mm guns that can spit out 625 rounds a minute. It looks like a spindly insect, if one can imagine an insect fifty-eight feet long that weighs 12,000 pounds. Inside, it holds a two-man crew, the only volitional elements in an otherwise mercilessly efficient machine. On this day, in July 2007, two Apaches are flying over Baghdad in what an investigation will later identify as Operation ILAAJ, *the clearance of Zone 30.*

The woman and her son probably don't realize they live in Zone 30.

The tactical term for the operation is *enemy engagement by aviation,* and what the *Crazyhorse* crew does here will eventually turbocharge a new kind of citizen engagement and will put a twenty-two-year-old army intelligence analyst who isn't even deployed yet in a military prison for thirty-five years.

And it's all recorded by the Apache's camera.


The video begins as the Apache gunner sights a group of men standing in a loose assemblage near a courtyard. They're *males of military age,* the technical term for fair game. The gunner thinks he sees a weapon. *Fucking prick.* He doesn't realize that what looks like an AK-47 is actually a camera with a long telephoto lens, or that the man who's just slung it over his shoulders is a cameraman with Reuters. A second Reuters cameraman is similarly misidentified a moment later; then several other men walk into the shot. Two of them actually are carrying AK-47s. They move in a manner that suggests they aren't aware they're under observation.

Meanwhile, the crosshairs float across the landscape.

The crew is antsy. *Have five to six individuals with AK-47s. Request permission to engage.* They're monitoring the pictures, worried they might lose the moment. *I'm gonna . . . I can't get 'em now because they're behind that building.* There's something serious at stake—troops on the ground have been taking intermittent fire in the area from unidentified individuals for much of the day—but at this distance it seems like a video game, with hidden threats popping up in different places. It takes nerve, skill, and a high level of alertness to take an enemy down.

It's probably a lot like what they did as kids in their living rooms.

The Reuters cameraman peeks around a building. He's pointing his camera lens at something. *All right, we got a guy with an RPG.* The telephoto lens has just morphed into a rocket-propelled grenade launcher. Permission to engage is granted.

*Light 'em all up!*

Plumes of smoke and dust momentarily obscure the scene. The gunner seems to be satisfied. *All right, hahaha, I hit 'em.* His official pronouncement is more measured, like a code called in an ER. *All right, we just engaged all eight individuals.* A moment later, another spontaneous admission: *Oh yeah, look at those dead bastards.* His crewmate acknowledges the kill—*Nice*—and the gunner responds. *Thank you.*

But it's not over. A wounded man is moving on the street. The crew operates under constraints, rules of engagement, which require a triggering action on the part of a target.

*Come on, buddy. All you gotta do is pick up a weapon.*

There's no weapon near him. It's clear from the video that he can hardly move. He's crawling to what he must hope is safety but he's not going to make it, not if this crew can help it.

*Come on, let us shoot!*

At that moment a vehicle drives into view. Three unarmed men jump out to assist the wounded man. They might be good Samaritans, they might be sinister, they might be both, it's hard to tell from 1,600 meters. The men start to haul the limp man into the van.

Then black smoke. Nothing's moving now.

*Oh yeah, look at that. Right through the windshield!*

*Location of bodies, Mike Bravo five-four-five-eight-eight-six-one-seven.*

In a matter of minutes a ground unit arrives and two small children are discovered in the van, wounded but still alive. Their father has been killed. The *Crazyhorse* crew is informed.

*Damn . . . it's their fault for bringing their kids into a battle.*

One of the soldiers scoops the little girl up. He's agitated. He'll later leave the military and try to lose himself in alcohol and self-loathing, this incident his own personal tipping point, the one memory he can't will away.

More concretely, he won't forget the smell at the scene. *I don't even know how to describe it.* It's a toxic mix of body parts and munitions, something an Apache crew will never experience. But for now the nightmares haven't yet begun and he's hell-bent on getting the kids to a medical facility. That's the kind of thing he thought he signed up for.

*We're America, John Wayne, we wear the white hats.*


But it wasn't 1944 anymore, and war wasn't just hell, like in the old days, it was worse. Without mass mobilization, your high school buddy wasn't likely to join the service alongside you. Prominent figures wouldn't fight either; no Jimmy Stewarts or Joe DiMaggios would be signing up. You'd be deployed multiple times while those back in the States lived comfortably in the cocoon of their own lives.

You'd see things. Maybe you'd do things.

Over time it would become harder to figure out what you were fighting for, if you ever thought about it at all.

Soldiers in this new battle environment needed new tools to cope.

The military had begun to develop something it called Resilience Training to counter the stresses of modern service. New technologies could greatly improve upon the motivational films of an earlier era. Virtual reality scenarios could now put soldiers in the field, in the middle of the action, in a Humvee itself, alongside lifelike avatars that moved and talked like them.

Some of them even cursed.

In one such animation an officer in fatigues materializes as the GIs freeze in the frame. He speaks directly to whoever's watching, a ghostly guide to the underworld of modern war. He talks them through a typical situation in the field, where a villager lying on the road might be friendly, might just need water, or might blow you up if you get too close. Captain Branch, as he's called, offers play-by-play commentary, peppered with slang. It's meant to be relatable to young soldiers. But it's not sugarcoated.

*Twisted crap happens all the time here.*

*What you've learned from every good and decent person in your life is sometimes gonna have to go on the back burner.*

*The right thing to do in San Diego or Charlotte or Where-the-hell-am-I Idaho could get you killed here.*

*There are no easy answers here.*

*This ain't no war movie.*

Except sometimes it seemed like one.

In the final moments of the Apache video the crew moves on to what looks like an abandoned building. Military-age males have been sighted inside. *Crazyhorse* gets permission to fire.

*There it goes! Look at that bitch light up!*

A bystander walks past the building at that moment. Wrong place, wrong time. He gets blown into oblivion.

*Roger, building destroyed. Engaged with three Hellfire missiles.*

The Apache video would be filed away on a military server until it resurfaced in 2009, part of a training session at Forward Operating Base Hammer in Iraq. An analyst was learning how to identify weapons systems. After the lesson, she and a few others watched the video again. They talked idly about the camera lens mix-up, whether they would have made the same mistake. They didn't get into the ethics of the situation.

Debating moral ambiguities wasn't job one, and Captain Branch wasn't around.

One soldier in the group had seen a lot of what he called *war porn* during his deployment, but to him this was different, more disturbing, harder to shake off. He brooded about it. He thought the public should know what was happening in its name, see some of the twisted stuff for themselves.

*I wanted the American public to know that not everyone in Iraq and Afghanistan are targets that need to be neutralized.*

He had an idea.

In addition to videos, analysts in his position had routine access to thousands of top secret documents, an *eyes-only* view of the sometimes disturbing ways in which American warfare and diplomacy were conducted behind closed doors.

He could make that material available for examination to anyone.

The technical term for the new capability was *crowd sourcing*, a tool that amplified voices and perspectives by fostering a kind of collective scrutiny. A hive mind. Information could be distributed over the Internet or social media and shared in a variety of different venues; collaborative vetting could occur; the public could decide for itself what was important. Anybody could become an analyst.

They wouldn't have to take someone like Walter Cronkite's word for it anymore.

He first offered the material to *The Washington Post* and *The New York Times*, in something of a retro reflex. But they weren't interested in another Daniel Ellsberg.

Going old school wouldn't work.

He then contacted a little-known online entity called WikiLeaks, a self-described *intelligence agency for the people*. It was said to welcome the kind of information he could offer. He sent the unedited Apache footage, followed by action memoranda, state department cables, and a multitude of other primary source documents.

No sense holding back.

On April 5, 2010, WikiLeaks unveiled a seventeen-minute version of the video at a news conference at the National Press Club. It was essentially a highlights reel (the woman walking with her son didn't make the cut). *Collateral Murder*, as it was titled, would subsequently be viewed more than sixteen million times online and would engender intense debate. A senior government official objected to criticisms of the Apache crew; out of context, it was like *looking at war through a soda straw*. Others saw clear evidence of war crimes.

To many, the leak itself was the outrage.

If nothing else, it was painfully apparent that it had become increasingly difficult to wall off information in this new age. The Internet was a sieve. Maybe it didn't even make sense to try. As the founder of WikiLeaks observed:

*The best way to keep a secret is never to have it.*

Pfc. Bradley Edward Manning joined the army in 2007. There was nothing in his outward manner to suggest the uproar he would soon create; he was, by his own admission, the kind of person who was easily overlooked (in a typical war movie, he would have been the quiet guy in the corner with glasses). It took him longer than usual to get through boot camp, given physical frailties, but he refused to be chaptered out. He wanted to go to college someday and he needed the GI Bill.

In the meantime, the army gave him the means to explore a fledging interest in global affairs.

Manning became a 35-Foxtrot intelligence analyst, or *35-Fox.* Command was blind without the almost pointillist images that analysts created of the *battle space,* bits of information about the enemy that meant little in isolation but could be woven together into something called *situational awareness.* SA could be distilled into crisp PowerPoint presentations. It was challenging. It took skill and some imagination to create a work product with predictive power.

At Manning's court-martial, an army captain characterized the hundreds of 35-Foxes he'd supervised over the years as *high maintenance:* smart, edgy around authority, feeling superior to just about everybody else. In a sense, the grandiosity that Manning's army psychiatrist diagnosed after his arrest wasn't a bug but a feature of an effective 35-Fox.

Like *Top Gun,* without Tom Cruise.

—

No one ever questioned Manning's proficiency. He was a natural, 10 out of 10 in data mining. *I looked anywhere and everywhere for information.* He liked sifting through data sources and he loved technology. (On October 3, 2009, at 4:03 a.m., his Facebook page marked a milestone: *Bradley Manning celebrates his recent acquisition of a 13" MacBook Pro.* Three weeks earlier, at 8:24 p.m.: *Bradley Manning is getting a little tired of pinging major ISPs at 750m/sec. Hopefully Iraq will have faster internet.*) A supervisor in theater marveled at the system Manning had devised to track everything he collected: files, directories, subfiles, subdirectories, redundancies, all designed to frame and filter the flood of information a curious researcher could uncover. To the Chief it was hats off, say what you will.

*I just never seen an analyst that kept that many reports.*

Manning's team leader also testified to his standout skills: *he was very fluent in anything computer. He spoke their language.* It was a language that needed translating for most everyone else. The presiding judge at trial asked a computer expert to explain what a *hard shutdown* of a computer was (she was told it involved pulling the plug); an FBI agent testified that he could use the Internet and knew what a Tweet was, but didn't know how to delete one; a soldier testified that analysts played *a little ball popping game* when things were slow, but she didn't know if it was an *executable file,* or why that might be important; his roommate told the court he had no idea why Manning would need blank CD-RW disks, much less the stack he kept in his quarters. *I thought it was weird since he had an iPod* (no one burned disks anymore). One of the trial attorneys was thrown by a witness's attempt to explain crowd sourcing, a concept as foreign to him as the cloud.

*So really it's more about the—that was a lot of—I was trying to follow along. But really it's more, about—really how information is, what, shared among—*

It seemed so complicated. Hard to keep pace. Kids these days.

But the divide wasn't really intergenerational any longer. Advances in technologies had begun to outstrip most everyone's capacity to understand them. Computer networks, weapons systems, even new cars that didn't need keys seemed increasingly opaque.

Some time later another leaker, Edward Snowden, would aver that he didn't have any special skills: *I'm just another guy*. But neither Snowden nor Manning were ordinary; the technologies they navigated with ease mystified most everyone else.

They knew how to harness the great power that most people just played with.


As a consequence, Manning was able to download and encrypt sensitive data without detection. But even he couldn't process hundreds of thousands of classified documents manually (that would have taken forever, like Ellsberg photocopying seven thousand pages of Pentagon Papers one at a time). He used automated programs like Wget and Base64 to collect the documents he would eventually pass on to WikiLeaks.

All he had to do was set the machinery in motion.

After he was finished, he initiated a *7-pass disk erase* of his laptop. That procedure took three hours and forty-eight minutes to complete. It would fool casual observers; only a specialist in computer forensics could determine that Manning had compromised 700,000 classified documents over seven months. He wouldn't be able to hide a single keystroke from someone like that, someone who could reconstruct the *Mike Delta Five hash, secure-hash-algorithm-one* trail of digital evidence. But it would have taken anyone else forever to find out.

—

As it happened, it was Manning himself who accelerated the discovery. By the time the WikiLeaks video came out he was, as he put it, *pretty desperate for some non-isolation.* He contacted a hacker he'd read about. The two strangers friended each other on Facebook, and started to talk in a private chat room. They had something in common—both could do almost anything with a network connection, and each had grappled with questions of sexuality. (That information would subsequently provoke great interest among the public, but it was only part of what kept Manning up at night now.) *Bradass87*—his chat nom de plume—needed to unburden himself.

It turned out he wasn't just a technician. He had a code, jerry-rigged but genuine.

> *if you saw incredible things, awful things—things that belonged in the public domain and not on some server stored in a dark room in Wash DC—what would you do?*

It was risky to disclose his deepest secrets to someone he didn't really know, even half a world away. He was nervous.

> *I can't believe what I'm confessing to you :(*

The frowny face was appropriate. His new Facebook friend called the FBI and Manning was immediately arrested on base in Iraq.

*United States v. Manning* took twelve weeks to argue before a military judge.

The government wanted the court to comprehend the scale of the disclosures over Manning's seven-month deployment.

*That's 100,000 documents per month, 3,300 documents per day, 138 documents per hour, and more than two documents every minute.*

To the prosecution Manning was an anarchist, with evil intent, a soldier who had subverted military values and jeopardized national security; to the defense he was a confused idealist, *22 years young,* a kid who just wanted to make the world better. What he had done was serious, but he never intended harm. And he was struggling with gender identity issues. That wasn't a pass, but it was important context.

Manning's own view was more complicated.

*i dont believe in good guys versus bad guys anymore.*

He was pronounced guilty of nineteen of the twenty-two charges.

After his sentencing Bradley Edward Manning declared he was transgender and wished from that moment on to be known as a woman. He took a new name and began to serve thirty-five years.

Seven years later, Chelsea Elizabeth Manning was released from Fort Leavenworth, her sentence commuted by the president. She had expressed remorse and wanted to move on. She made one last admission that she hoped would finally set her free.

*I am not Bradley Manning. I really never was.*

# 3

On April 13, 2017, the United States military dropped a Massive Ordnance Air Bomb Blast over an ISIS tunnel compound in Nangarhar Province, Afghanistan. MOAB, nicknamed the Mother of All Bombs, was the nation's most powerful nonnuclear weapon: thirty feet long, 21,600 pounds, capable of leveling an area equal to nine city blocks.

It was the first time the $16 million weapon had been used in combat.

The blast killed just thirty-six suspected members of ISIS, but its main purpose was widely considered to be psychological, a demonstration of shock and awe signaling to the world that the United States remained a formidable foe.

This time the Pentagon got ahead of the story, releasing its own cockpit video of the strike on YouTube the next day.

The Doomsday Clock was moved to 2.5 minutes to midnight.


Some suspected that a new president was just warming up with MOAB. He had expressed interest in the nation's nuclear stockpile as a candidate (*Why can't we use them?*) and after the third iteration of the question they began to wonder if he was serious.

Ideas that had lain dormant for decades emerged once again, dusted off for new generations who had no memory of ducking under desks as children. One of those ideas held that apocalyptic thinking was old-fashioned, even melodramatic.

That hypothesis had first been broached in a notorious 1980 think tank article titled *Victory is Possible*. It was essentially a pitch for the survivability of nuclear war. *Self-deterrence* was a sign of weakness; no world power should take anything off the table. Indeed, the United States ought to develop new low-yield tactical nukes, weapons nimble enough to be employed in situations that fell short of outright obliteration, in wars that could be survived, even won.

We might lose twenty million people, but we could rebuild.

The notion that a nuclear conflict could be contained was derided as fringe thinking in 1980, but the idea (and its architect, now an adviser to the president) resurfaced thirty-eight years later, like a bad penny, in the official *Nuclear Posture Review of 2018*, successor to the more circumspect *NPR* of 2010. Threats had proliferated, adjustments were necessary, low-yield nukes offered a more nuanced range of responses, and they ought to have been built much earlier.

The document still reflexively declared that only extreme circumstances would prompt the nation (in the person of the president) to deploy this awesome weapon for the third time in history.

*Nevertheless, if deterrence fails, the United States will strive to end any conflict at the lowest level of damage possible.*

In the new thinking, Armageddon could be micromanaged.


*The Washington Post* ran a piece in January 2018 posing a newly current question: "What should you do if a nuclear bomb is heading your way?" The article seemed to encourage flexibility, options, resourcefulness.

*You may have about 10 to 15 seconds to do something.*

It provided a helpful link to FEMA, the new version of the Civil Defense Administration of the 1950s. FEMA had produced slick brochures updating the old tunes—*Prepare, Survive, Be Safe*— in exhortations that could now be downloaded as pdfs. No more booklets sent out by snail mail.

Basements were again touted, as in the old days, but any concrete enclosure would do (a nod to the reality that subterranean spaces had since gone out of fashion). Readers were advised that nuclear weapons were no longer massive; they could appear in the form of *a small portable device carried by an individual.* The scientists had always known that, but now the general public was put on notice. Also, citizens were cautioned that detonation of a nuclear device could interfere with communications: *cell phone, text messaging, and internet services may be disrupted.*

If you still had a landline, you already knew the drill.

In the meantime, those whose Internet capabilities were intact could go to the interactive site NUKEMAP, plug in any Google Maps location across the world, hit the red button, and watch as the blast radius of various weapons widened, the concentric circles darkening one's own neighborhood or someone else's city. The simulations were triggered by a sophisticated set of variables, among them airbursts, surface bursts, fallout (tied to wind speed), thermal radiation rings, ionizing radiation rings, and variously sized mushroom clouds.

For those who wished to dive further into the weeds, the site estimated the effects of different radiation doses: 100 rems would cause sickness and increased lifetime cancer risk, while 600 rems would cause 80% mortality, even with medical care. At 5,000 rems, nothing would matter anymore.

It all depended on what circle you were in.

Armchair strategists could choose from over thirty differ-ent nuclear yields, measured in kilotons or megatons, from early A-bombs (Little Boy over Hiroshima, fifteen kilotons, or Fat Man over Nagasaki, twenty kilotons), to the far more powerful H-bombs tested by India, Pakistan, North Korea, Russia, China, and the United States itself. Castle Bravo, a fifteen-megaton U.S. bomb, would result in possibly five million fatalities if detonated over New York City; Tsar Bomba, a fifty-megaton weapon tested by the USSR, might kill almost eight million people in the same area.

Better to be hit by the device North Korea tested in 2017, a mod-est 150 kilotons, with 500,000-plus fatalities, or *a crude terrorist weapon*, the kind carried in a suitcase, for 5,730 fatalities.

NUKEMAP went online in 2012; within eight years it had logged millions of virtual detonations.

Meanwhile, readers of the *Post* article had their own ideas about What You Should Do if a Nuclear Bomb Is Heading Your Way. They spoke to each other in the public square of the comments sec-tion, a virtual space unavailable in an earlier era.

*Try not to be in the wrong place at the wrong time . . . Grab a six pack, head to the roof of the tallest building around, and enjoy the view while it lasts . . . I would pray to God it detonated over my head . . . Who in their right mind would want to survive a nuclear attack?*

The Doomsday Clock was moved to two minutes to midnight.

—

By 2020 most people weren't worried about disappearing in a nuclear cloud. Instead, the focus of dread became predator bugs, a vicious subset of the everyday viral entities that were, essentially, everywhere.

No one had been thinking about bugs just a while earlier; soon enough, no one would be thinking about anything else.

The Novel Corona-19 Virus (technically SARS-CoV-2, soon to be known simply as COVID), having seen much of the Far East and Europe, was on its way to America.

A small group of American epidemiologists and health professionals had begun to monitor the virus informally as it moved across China. They were not prone to panic, but it didn't take much imagination to see what was on the horizon.

It helped to confer with one another. No one else would understand. *Community transmission, surge capacity, targeted mitigation measures, NPI, $R_O$, PPE, CFR*—the arcane idioms of their field were all shorthand for a situation that could easily spin out of control.

Their deliberations were captured in eighty pages of leaked e-mails obtained by *The New York Times,* the subject line "Red Dawn Rising."

Those who knew their movies knew that wasn't good.

To the experts, the need for a rapid response was clear and immediate.

*We cannot prepare the future by acting in the future.*

The idea that such a response might not be forthcoming from American officials was the stuff of a waking nightmare.

*I couldn't sleep . . . This is unbelievable . . . we are so far behind the curve . . .*

It was a five-alarm, all-hands-on-deck, the-call-is-coming-from-inside-the-house kind of emergency, but no one else was paying attention.

*I'm not sure that folks understand what's coming . . . infection will spread like fire . . . people are carrying the virus everywhere.*

One researcher did some back-of-the-envelope estimates. He ran the numbers, switched up the scenarios, altered variables, plugged in different values, trying to arrive at a different outcome. No such luck.

*This is going to be bad.*

It was just two weeks after the first U.S. COVID fatality had been reported.

The eighty pages of e-mails, from January to late March, could be summed up in two concise sentences.

*COVID is like a storm coming to our communities . . . We know what works; we just need the will to do it.*

One of the few women in the group expressed the enormity of what was unfolding in terms even a layperson could understand.

*This is so very sad.*

Most of the nation, like much of the world, was eventually put on lockdown, its businesses, schools, and shops shuttered by individual states and cities. Forty-four million people were abruptly unemployed, losing their employer-based health insurance in the worst health crisis in a century.

Clamorous headlines could hardly keep up with the ominous developments.

*STATES DROWNING BENEATH A DELUGE OF JOB LOSS CLAIMS; SALES AT U.S. STORES HIT "CATASTROPHIC" DEPTHS.*

The all-caps treatment, commonly equated with screaming in print, seemed an appropriate response to national collapse.

Think *Titanic, Hindenburg,* 1929, Jonestown, and Carter-era gas shortages, and then think of something even worse.

That was the only rational recourse available to citizens when the federal government itself denied the seriousness of the situation.

Images of the COVID bug were newly ubiquitous. It looked menacing, a ball with spikes that punctured healthy cell walls like an ancient weapon, searching for a weakness, its lethality packed into a sphere less than 0.1 microns in size.

You would never see it coming.

While reactions to imminent nuclear annihilation had been fatalistic *(Grab a six pack),* the response to this new threat was fearful.

Just speaking to someone, laypeople were told, could propel thousands of invisible droplets into the air, the mist dispersing in all directions. Coughs were worse. And sneezes were explosive, 40,000 droplets expelled in a spray that traveled at warp speed wherever it wanted.

No one yet knew how long the bugs survived on paper, metal, cloth, or in aerosol form.

You'd have to be a reader of the *Journal of Fluid Mechanics* to figure that out.

Ameliorative measures were advised. *Wear a mask. Wash your hands. Practice social distancing.*

The president himself proposed off the cuff therapeutic protocols—wait for warm weather, inject disinfectants, cross your fingers.

Who really knew what might work?

In the absence of definitive information, with no coordinated national response to rely upon, no treatment, no vaccine, and nothing but unanswered questions, worriers looked to one another online for advice. No hedging there.

*Treat all people as if they are infected and all surfaces as if they are dirty or compromised.*

Even six-packs would have to be sanitized.


Households provisioned themselves like combatants gone to ground. Supply lines were overwhelmed as Clorox, Lysol spray, toilet paper, and nonmedical masks vanished from the marketplace (even Amazon abandoned two-day delivery for the duration). Grocery shopping became an ordeal, hoarding the strategy of choice for those who had the means and space to stock up.

Grocery clerks were dubbed *essential workers* by a newly grateful nation.

Slightly more alarming were the critical shortages of essential medical supplies that the experts had warned about for years. Hospital workers lacked Personal Protective Equipment (masks, paper gowns, gloves) and ICUs didn't have enough ventilators. States vied with one another for scarce shipments from abroad, bidding the costs up for everyone. Some worried that the stockpiles of equipment necessary for the eventual vaccine (syringes, vials, cotton swabs) had been depleted years earlier and never replaced, contrary to the urgent recommendations of the high-level pandemic response playbook prepared in 2016.

The sixty-nine-page playbook offered step-by-step protocols taken from the Ebola experience, its purpose to equip governmental leaders with *decision-making tools* to get ahead of any outbreak.

It was ignored by the Trump administration.

In New York City, early epicenter of the outbreak, refrigerated trucks were parked outside hospitals to accommodate the overflow of COVID fatalities. Sirens wailed 24/7 across the boroughs.

City dogs began to howl in unison with the whine.

In a matter of days the Army Corps of Engineers erected temporary field hospitals in a city that had run out of beds and ventilators. A private charity put up a tent hospital in Central Park. The thousand-bed USNS *Comfort* was dispatched to New York harbor.

Similar scenes were inevitably repeated across the country.

It seemed to be the worst outbreak ever. Except, as the experts knew, it wasn't.

Americans had forgotten about the Great Pandemic of 1918, how something as seemingly benign as a seasonal illness (*Get your flu shot*) had once been life-threatening. Almost no one living had experienced that cataclysmic event. Those who did would have been infants, spared awareness of worldwide contagion and war.

Wartime military mobilization had diverted a third of America's doctors from civilian life. Hundreds of thousands of troops had been crammed into ships and camps, all what a later age would call ideal *vectors of transmission*. Workers in war industries were crowded together as well.

First responders of the era did what they could in their local communities.

The 1918 flu bugs were so virulent that many people died within days of infection.

Protocols were quickly developed to mitigate the contagion. Citizens were instructed to avoid crowds and walk to work when possible. Streetcars were sprayed with disinfectants. Spitting on floors and sidewalks was outlawed; the use of spittoons was discouraged. Night schools and theaters were closed and public gatherings banned.

Anyone who fell ill, authorities announced, should go to bed, stay away from others, and open the windows to encourage air circulation.

Everyone was expected to wear a mask. The *San Luis Obispo Daily Telegram* of November 1, 1918 (*60c a month and worth it*) publicly shamed those who refused to observe the edict in an article on the front page (*you think laws are made for other people but not for you*).

News of the Kaiser's imminent abdication made the front page as well, but the continuing scourge of the nation was accorded the most attention (*Nine new cases of flu reported this morning*).

One World War was about to end; the other was still raging.

By the time it was over, after three waves of infection spanning twenty-four months, fifty million people had died, 675,000 of them Americans. Young people in their twenties had proven most vulnerable to the virus.

Life expectancy in the United States dropped by twelve years.


On the hundredth anniversary of the Great Pandemic the *American Journal of Epidemiology* noted that medical and governmental professionals now had *a myriad of tools for pandemic response planners*. Science had made great strides in the interim.

It was 2018, after all.

But those on the COVID e-mail chain in 2020 were less sanguine about strides.

All they could do now was watch, horrified, as a preventable catastrophe took its course.

*This is exactly what happened in 1918. Unfortunately, we have to learn some lessons again and again.*


Three months into the COVID pandemic over 100,000 Americans had fallen victim to the virus. One of them was a New Yorker named Jack Draifinger. Jack's brother, Alex, put some thoughts down for family and friends to mark the moment:

*My brother Jack will be a statistic but to us he was a man that is special. Jack was one of those souls that was close to the earth, the common man, his family, his community. He was the warmest, communicative and gentle person one could know.*

He could have been speaking for 100,000 other families, each coping with sudden, singular loss.

—

In late May, a few months on, the COVID crisis abruptly disappeared from public consciousness.

An unarmed black man had been murdered by police on a street in Minneapolis, the video going viral like a fever breaking. The death of George Floyd reignited national resistance to racial injustice. Millions joined together to march, insisting *black lives matter*, the outrage only intensifying as weeks passed. It became the largest wave of public unrest in living memory.

The sound of sirens morphed into the buzzing of police helicopters overhead.

The secretary of defense declared the streets of American cities *battle spaces.*

Police forces had been in paramilitary mode since the 1960s, the friendly cop with a pistol supplanted by SWAT teams and shields. Years of war in the Mideast had generated surplus hardware available to localities across the country. The equipment was formally allocated through the Law Enforcement Support Office (LESO) of the Department of Defense. President Obama had canceled the program but his successor had reinstated it.

Any policy that generated an acronym, after all, was probably meant to be permanent.

Tensions between protestors and police came to a head one evening in Lafayette Square, the open space across from the White House that had accommodated peaceful public assembly for generations. The president wanted a path cleared for a brisk walk and photo op. Marchers were shelled with tear gas canisters and pepper spray projectiles. The crowd dispersed, on cue, the shocked young people scrambling in all directions.

They wouldn't have been alive the last time a National Guard force fired on students. But that moment in Lafayette Square would become infamous, like Kent State in 1970, with a twenty-first-century twist: the respiratory distress caused by tear gas exacerbated the effects of COVID.


A forbidding eight-foot-tall black metal fence appeared overnight around the White House and the park.

The barrier constituted, in one sense, an inadvertent commentary on the contradictions of the carceral state, the president imprisoning himself in a country with the highest incarceration rate in the world.

Americans were beginning to learn that systemic conditions implicated everyone.

The fence was soon festooned with colorful posters from the protests. It was a subversive reclamation of space that had arisen spontaneously, prompting curators from the Smithsonian (still on lockdown) to review the displays with an eye to acquisition. History was unfolding as the nation watched. Its markers ought to be preserved for the future.

A new generation might, in time, look back to 2020 as a defining moment in their lives, as their elders had been changed by the convulsive energies of the 1960s.

Even the unlikeliest nooks and crannies of the culture were swept up in the moment.

Trendy lifestyle websites that had recently featured recipes and hand-thrown ceramic mugs at $46 apiece were now presenting their readers with anti-racist reading lists.

Some scoffed at fashionable corporate pieties (*Could you stop already with the virtue signaling and just publish cooking content?*) but others welcomed what they considered a long overdue reckoning with racial injustice.

Pieces showcasing *10 French Flea Market Finds I Can't Stop Thinking About* could wait; newly engaged readers were offered, instead, articles like *5 Ways White People Can Be Helpful Right Now.*

Activism, if embraced, could itself be considered a lifestyle.

Over one thousand public health professionals wrote an open letter supporting the Black Lives Matter marches. Many of them had earlier condemned assemblies of agitated white supremacists in Midwestern statehouses, given the dangers of COVID contagion. They felt it necessary to explain the apparent contradiction.

*White supremacy is a lethal public health issue that predates and contributes to COVID-19.*

They noted the dramatic disparities in health outcomes of communities of color. The indices had moved too long in the wrong direction: lower life expectancy, higher maternal and infant mortality, chronic health ailments, poor housing, limited access to healthcare, all contributing to the toxicity of living in a racist society.

It was predictable that people of color would be disproportionately affected by the COVID virus.

Maybe these marchers, by risking their own safety, were calling attention to a larger public health problem as well.

The logic didn't satisfy everyone but it made some sense.

Many of the marchers had themselves already made the connection, distilling socioeconomic and medical complexities into one immediate message that fit neatly onto a poster.

*Racism is a virus.*

By that time, several months into the lockdown, much of America was itching to reopen, visit older at-risk relatives, get a haircut, eat again in restaurants. Some who still had jobs wanted to return to the office. Others who had lost jobs wanted to sit at a bar. Many just wanted to take off their masks.

A new term of art arose to address the phenomenon: *Covidiots.*

The experts were almost certain another wave was coming, anyone who knew their 1918 history could predict that a subsequent bout of the virus might be even worse. The killer was still out there, impervious to a potential host's impatience. By one informed estimate new cases could spike to 100,000 per day if mitigation measures weren't observed.

But it was time to tune the experts out. Worrying about the virus, like worrying about nuclear weapons or climate change, was exhausting. America decided to change the channel.

The Doomsday Clock was set to one hundred seconds to midnight.

*Secrets*

*Secrecy is sometimes defined as a sly or cautious stealthiness, a desire to hide or deceive. Expressions have arisen over the years to rebuff those who try to meddle in someone else's affairs: 'keep your nose out of it,' 'mind your own beeswax.'*

*Neither expression is much help anymore.*

*It used to be said that everyone had secrets. Now that belief seems sentimental, given that boundaries are porous, technology is intrusive, and the public confessional is open to anyone with access to social media.*

*Still, it might be instructive to return to a time when those who wanted to reveal something about themselves really had to work at it, and those who wanted to snoop had their work cut out as well.*

# I

*Someone has torn up a letter and thrown it away. Picking up the pieces, one finds that many of them can be fitted together.*

—Sei Shonagon, *The Pillow Book*,
tenth century CE

Things she disliked: dogs that howled in daytime, the last rain of the year, lovers who failed to show up when expected, loud drunken louts, carriages that creaked, babies that cried at inopportune moments, mice, mosquitoes. Things that pleased her: a night with a clear moon, a thin wisp of cloud, a clever poem, forgotten messages from a man she used to love. Sometimes, she confessed to her notebook: *It is very sinful of me, but I cannot help being pleased when someone I dislike has a bad experience.* At other times she was easier on herself, noting that she usually wished only the best for those she loved. Very little escaped her attention: she recorded violations of etiquette, presumptions of self-importance, the shrunken figure of a sumo wrestler after a defeat. She also studied spiderwebs, a trifle that most in her circle considered unworthy of notice.

She was unrepentant.

*I am the sort of person who approves of what others abhor and detests the things they like.*


Her name may have been Sei Shonagon. She might have been born in 965 CE. She almost certainly served as a lady-in-waiting to the Empress Sadako for ten years, and was probably favored for her quick wit. It was the empress who gave her the paper to write upon. *The Pillow Book* may or may not have been intended for a wider audience, but word got out.

Her great contemporary, Murasaki Shikibu, author of *The Tale of Genji*, wrote of her rival in her own diary. *She is gifted, yet if one has to sample each interesting thing that comes along, people are bound to regard one as frivolous. How can things turn out well for such a woman?*

As it happened, things would turn out well enough: over time, Shonagon would be judged a great prose stylist, inspiring a new genre of Japanese literature, and her idiosyncratic work would continue to be read a thousand years after her death.


*The Pillow Book* consists of three hundred disconnected paragraphs and 164 lists, a taxonomy of stray moods and observations. *Things That Make One's Heart Beat Faster. Things That Have Lost Their Power. Shameful Things. Awkward Things. Things That Fall from the Sky.*

She admitted to the miscellany, even reveled in it. A succession of translators would declare it unsystematic, haphazard, bizarre, but for her its organizing principle could be distilled to a single precept.

*Everything that I have seen and felt is included.*

Nothing of her life is known after her service to the empress ended. No one can determine where she lived or when she died or how she spent her days until that moment. All that remains of Sei Shonagon is the document she left behind, its pieces to be fitted together, in some fashion, by its readers.

She would have undoubtedly found that a Pleasing Thing.

In the book's last sequence, she admits to a reluctance to put down her pen.

*It is getting so dark that I can scarcely go on writing; and my brush is all worn out. Yet I should like to add a few things before I end.*

She knew that even a tell-all could never be complete.

# 2

*It is no easy job writing about nothing.*
—Arthur Inman, *Diary,* 1919–1963

For over forty years he scribbled seventeen million words, enough so that Harvard University Press had to abridge his life's work into two volumes of 1,661 pages before publication. As a young man he had abandoned his first epic, *The Life of Cortez,* for the more familiar expanse of his own psyche. (Apparently, like Montaigne, he had concluded that he knew only one subject well enough to write about it.) He subsequently produced 155 notebooks about nothing, delineating in meticulous detail the world of a wealthy semi-invalid. The panoramic novels of Dos Passos, which he admired, gave him something to aim at.

*I want to put down what I see, perceive, think, feel, all in the most realistic yet most artistic way of which I am capable.*

Born in 1895 in the Deep South, Arthur Crew Inman settled in

Boston as an adult. There he could find, if he wished, another literary lineage, other New Englanders whose work might inspire him. Emerson, for one, had famously exhorted the ordinary man to heed his own counsel; *he dismisses without notice his thought, because it is his.* Or Henry Adams, in his *Education*, self-effacing, like Inman never sure whether his work was worthless or inspired. But Inman instead saw something of himself in the figure of Benedict Arnold. Treason aside, Arnold had been driven by a desire that was only too familiar.

*He didn't want to be a nobody.*

The diarist, a recluse, paid people to come talk with him about their lives. His obliging wife placed the solicitations in the newspaper. He had no interest in talking to her; she was, in his estimation, *a dead personality.* The notebooks make passing reference to hundreds of these *talkers* over the decades. Some became regulars of a sort, relating the ups and downs of their everyday experiences for a few dollars a day.

It must have been diverting to watch a wealthy eccentric waste his money.

Even in his sleep Inman was intrusive. He describes one night during which his dream-self flew about the city looking into windows. It was exhilarating, and something of a disappointment to wake up.

*So many secrets I saw, so many heard, all this morning forgotten.*


In 1945, after the A-bomb went off and the war ended, twenty-six years into his opus, he despaired about the future of his work. *What's the use? It will all be destroyed shortly, what I write, the civilization I live in, unless I mistake matters and trends.* His hope for fame would be obliterated if the diary never reached any readers.

The world was still standing when he passed away almost twenty years later.

Had he not been a man of means, his diary would surely have remained a family oddity stashed away in a basement. But he could pay for publication. The work was bequeathed to Harvard University, along with the funds to publish it.

The first edition is prefaced by a lengthy editor's introduction, in effect a user's guide to navigating the text. Even at two volumes, a fraction of the whole, the effort would tax the most well-intentioned reader.

Inman himself had anticipated the challenge.

*I delve back into my past and set down all the odds and ends I can remember so that in the fullness of time I shall have painted the parts of a connected frieze which you, dear readers of the future, will have to put together.*

Several approaches to the diary were suggested. It might be read as the case study of an eccentric, or a deep dive into one man's mind, or a social portrait of American life over decades, or a nonfiction novel. Or, all else failing, it might be advisable simply to surrender to a work *too huge and amorphous to classify.* An outpouring with no apparent pattern. A haystack without a needle. Odds and ends forever unconnected.

Or, as a twenty-first-century editor might put it, a massive data dump or Facebook feed.

# 3

*She says that Klara should never have married
Mike in the first place. Granted. But what is she
to do now?*

—Robert Shields, *Diary*,
Monday, April 18, 1994

The diary of Robert Shields, reverend and sometime teacher born
in 1918, clocks in at thirty-seven million words painstakingly com-
piled over twenty-five years, his waking life delineated in five-minute
increments. It took him four hours a day to record the data; he ro-
tated between six electric typewriters. He was careful not to priori-
tize entries or events; in the short run, his recollections might seem
banal, even inconsequential, but no one could foresee what would
truly matter in the long run.

Better not to leave anything out.

On that April day in 1994, in addition to fussing about Mike and Klara, Shields notes that he put two Stouffer's macaroni and cheese dinners into the oven at 6:30 p.m. and later, at 8:10 p.m., drank a twelve-ounce Pepsi while watching *Murder, She Wrote* on television. At 9:05, he interrupted the chronology, as if making a note to self.

*I wish I knew something. Anything would do.*

For an instant he seemed on the verge of a discovery, possibly something about the difference between knowledge and information, or whether a near infinite number of data points would ever add up to anything, in the end, but the moment passed.

It was time to get back to the typing.


Unlike earlier encyclopedic diarists, Shields lived in an era increasingly given to expansive self-disclosure. His obsessive practice piqued the interest of others. During a national radio interview he was asked if he had ever thought about walking away from the diary. The question seemed to surprise him.

*It would be like turning off my life.*

In 1997 he suffered a stroke and the Selectrics fell silent. (He had hoped that his wife would carry on, but she had never been much of an enthusiast.) He would live another ten years, the last 5,256,000 minutes of his life lost to posterity. The incomplete work was donated to Washington State University and, per his instructions, impounded for several decades.

As a consequence, curious readers won't learn what happened to Klara and Mike's marriage until the year 2049.

# 4

It would be natural enough to assume that only cranks, ne'er-do-wells, or nobodies become obsessive diarists; others, perhaps, lack the ego or the time to record their own lives with such zeal. In fact, fully functional and fairly busy people have engaged in the practice. Some are even known for other achievements.

Buckminster Fuller, futurist who conceived the geodesic dome and was shortlisted for the Nobel Prize, among many distinctions, also fretted about preserving the detritus generated in any given day of his life, storing every receipt, bill, award citation, personal note, or scrap even tangentially related to his own experience in a huge repository.

He had a vision. His collection, if comprehensive enough, would not be egocentric, or even personal; it would acquire a universality that could illuminate life in the twentieth century.

From that perspective, the undertaking was almost selfless.

Over sixty-six years Fuller collected 90,000 pounds of material. Eventually, the boxes were transported in massive trucks to a warehouse at Stanford University and stored, fodder for scholars and fans of the future. Like those before him, Fuller had fulfilled the prime directive of diarist-documentarians.

*I must put everything in it.*

# 5

*Total Recall is inevitable.*

—Gordon Bell, 2010

Worn brushes, stubby pencils, balky typewriters, unsympathetic relatives, dust-ridden boxes piled in garages; onerous hours spent collecting and cataloging, no days off, worry over warehouse space and eighteen-wheelers, embarrassment about guilty pleasures perhaps best undertaken in private.

Even the most dedicated diarist must have wished for an easier way to do the work.

It would take a techno geek like Gordon Bell to develop the dream of effortless recollection. He had been a pioneer of computing in the 1960s and had eventually gravitated to a research position with Microsoft. Over a long career he had seen mainframes that filled whole rooms shrink to the size of small boxes on a desk. He had outlived 8-track tapes, pagers, Betamax and VHS cassettes, disks, Zip drives, FTP, and MS-DOS, along with projects of his own that had been superseded.

He had also sifted through faded family pictures, tried to substantiate the unreliable recollections of loved ones, wondered whether he would pass on anything of his own life as his memories began to blur.

The thought of extinction disturbed him.

Still, there was no percentage in denial. Everything decayed. The latest devices were destined to become scraps of metal and silicon, just as the most robust bodies and minds would one day be reduced to scattered bits of biomatter.

Unless, given the will and the means, the two worlds could be bridged.

New devices were already in development—tiny cameras, microphones, and sensors could record data automatically. Increased computing power was coupled with exponentially expanded capacities for storage. The problem of maintaining viable equipment could be solved. Devices were already being embedded in the body. Artificial intelligence could one day be employed to create avatars that interacted with one's descendants.

And the cost curves were coming down.

He prepared a pitch. As an *extreme lifelogger*, with Microsoft's support, he could design an experiment in lifetime personal data storage and retrieval. He could test the new technologies on himself.

And, perhaps, avert his own obsolescence.


It wasn't just the Bell family that would benefit. Anyone could become a lifelogger, collect whatever they had seen, heard, or done, and it wouldn't, as in the past, consist only of inert piles of paper. Digital technology could capture the old stuff, but also do something new—capture interactions in real time. And track your location information over a lifetime. Only the thoughts in your head would remain unrecorded.

There would eventually be a huge payoff for the average person. *With the right software you will be able to mine your digital memory archive for patterns and trends that you could never uncover on your own.*

Because he was partnering with Microsoft, the developments might even be monetized. One could foresee practical applications. Need an alibi? Your personal archive will provide it. Mired in a *he said, she said* situation? Just pull up the encounter and see who's telling the truth. Strange flutter in your chest? The biosensors will have flagged it. No more undetected arrhythmias, no more health professionals hoarding data that was rightfully yours.

And all this information would fit into a single thumb drive one could put in a pocket.

Digital immortality might not appeal to everyone; there would always be those who chose to live off the grid, which in the twenty-first century amounted to a kind of death in itself. Privacy advocates might raise concerns (though that ship had long since sailed). Dystopians might recoil at a world in which nothing was off the record. But few others would be able to resist its ease and promise.

In any case, transformational technology was on the horizon, and those who understood that were going to exploit it. He wouldn't be the first to play with powerful new tools.

The real issue, Bell intimated, was more interesting, and it spoke to a philosophical problem that society as a whole would be wise to ponder.

*Is every digital life worth saving?*

He didn't consider the ancillary question: in a society that spied on its own citizens, would individuals be allowed to make such a decision for themselves?

# 6

*The intensity and complexity of life have ren-*
*dered necessary some retreat from the world*
    —Louis Brandeis, "The Right to Privacy,"
                                          1890

In his boyhood, anyone who wanted a photograph of himself had to pose, stiffly, for several minutes before a large bulky camera resting on a tripod. The stillness was unnatural, the immobility almost painful. No one took such a picture inadvertently, or on the spur of the moment, but only to mark special occasions in family or national life.

The formal images were mounted in homes and businesses across America.

By the time Louis Brandeis had become a young lawyer, later in the nineteenth century, *advances in the photographic art* had made it possible to take candid pictures without permission. Protopaparazzi ambushed socialites for images that ended up in news-papers, intruding upon *the sacred precincts of private life*. The pain of unwelcome publicity caused injury to the fundamental value of *an inviolate personality*. Ordinary people had *the right to be let alone*, and the dizzying pace of mechanical invention threatened that peace.

The language was nineteenth century, the malady all too modern.

In his seminal 1890 essay, and later as a justice on the Supreme Court, Brandeis laid down a new marker in modern life, *the right to privacy*, limning the parameters of a debate that would continue into the twenty-first century.


Subsequent courts, grappling with further technological develop-ments that might trigger Fourth Amendment protections, struggled to deploy analogies built upon earlier determinations.

Is a motorcycle like an automobile? Or a telephone booth like a private room? Or a wireless signal sent through the air like a land-line? Or an e-mail like a sealed letter? Or a cell phone an extension of the human body?

It was difficult enough to look at the present through the lens of the past, almost impossible to imagine the future. But Justice Brandeis, in 1928, was still worrying about threats to the private sphere almost forty years after he had first raised the alarm.

*Advances in the psychic and related sciences may bring means of exploring unexpressed beliefs, thoughts and emotions.*

He wouldn't live to see it, but he feared there might come a day when a retreat from the world was no longer possible.

# 7

Americans were crazy about secrets in the 1950s, if one could judge by the programs they were likely to watch each week. The popular game show *I've Got a Secret* premiered in 1952; its panelists were charged with interrogating guests who were hiding something. It might be an elderly man who as a five-year-old had witnessed Lincoln's assassination, or a little boy who had eaten his brother's bugs, or the meek engineer who stumped them all. He had invented *electronic television*, they learned, as a fourteen-year-old working in a garage.

The panelists might fumble, but the studio audience and *the folks at home* were always in on the secret.

A few years later, *To Tell the Truth* made its television debut. The rules were simple: three contestants claimed to be the same person, but two of them were lying. The panel was granted a limited number of questions to identify the impostors. Whatever the outcome, viewers learned that ordinary people who seemed guileless could lie as easily as anyone else.

One might conclude that a country recently blindsided by the atomic bomb would naturally suspect that secrets were everywhere, that nothing was as it seemed on the surface.

It wasn't just game shows that offered such diversion.

In 1954, in the first congressional hearing ever televised, Senator Joseph McCarthy conducted a public inquiry into the presence of subversives in American life. Communists were everywhere, it seemed, hidden throughout government, burrowing into radar facilities, atomic and hydrogen bomb plants, possibly ordinary homes. And the military. And schools. Even, perhaps, the very committee charged with ferreting them out.

His mission: to *lay the truth upon the table.*

It was riveting television – the operatic accusations, the relentless hectoring, the dramatic denouement when the phrase *Have you no decency, sir* entered the popular lexicon for the first time. Alert viewers could catch glimpses of the young Roy Cohn and Robert Kennedy in the hearing room. The public had grown familiar with easygoing inquisitions; McCarthy, with his fleshly scowl, offered a more sinister showmanship that was, in its way, just as entertaining.

He would eventually lose his audience, but not before appealing to *the average American* for help. He couldn't stem the *Red tide* by himself. There were still fellow travelers out there, in workplaces, the streets, the house next door, harboring terrible secrets.

It might be left to the folks at home to take up the search themselves.

In the meantime, the American government needed a means to gather and safeguard its own secrets in the postwar world. In 1952

President Truman created the National Security Agency by executive order, itself Top Secret. It was intended to consolidate disparate military intelligence departments into one über-entity.

The NSA was nicknamed No Such Agency by its staffers, a joke only those with a Need to Know could appreciate. Everyone outside the agency—the public, politicians, occasionally presidents—would be kept in the dark. Even twenty years on, a government official could confidently declare, *One has to search far and wide to find someone who has ever heard of the NSA.*

Americans also didn't know that much of their mail would be monitored over ensuing decades by the more familiar FBI and CIA. Millions of envelopes were photographed (collecting what a later era would term *metadata*) and thousands of letters opened and copied before being returned to the mailstream for delivery.

The three agencies were also variously reading telegrams, tapping phone lines, and identifying anti-government protestors.

They didn't seem much interested in diaries.

The intelligence triumvirate would maintain operational invisibility for over two decades, until the bipartisan Church Committee opened congressional hearings in the wake of Watergate and a new generation discovered the challenge of stripping secrets away.

# 8

*Black bag job, cover, safe house, watch list.* In the 1970s Americans learned a new language, replete with its own peculiar idioms. *Bug* was a noun and a verb; a *cut-out* an innocent-seeming intermediary between people who communicated on the sly. *Blown* meant one's *cover* was no longer operative. A *plausible denial* helped to throw others off track, especially if one was *a confusion agent* or a *source*.

And it was never good to be a *Target*.

The Church Committee, known formally as the Senate Select Committee to Study Governmental Operations with Respect to Intelligence Activities, convened in June 1975 to expose what its chairman, Senator Frank Church of Idaho, termed *insidious encroachments upon the liberties of American citizens*.

It was, he noted, the eve of the two hundredth birthday of the nation, an especially apt moment to revisit foundational creeds and values.

Senator Church framed the committee's work starkly. Mail Opening was just one of the dubious initiatives under investigation (while tracking activists, the Nixon administration had briefly considered a plan to put anti-war protestors into internment camps, among other alarming ideas). It was important that these unprecedented abuses not remain abstractions. Metaphors might help.

*This committee knows that the NSA is one gigantic set of earphones.* That language, while clear, evoked anodyne images of RadioShack.

*I cannot myself condone such Government snooping.* More pointed, but too polite.

*The NSA is a huge vacuum cleaner.* That image was more useful. Everyone had a vacuum at home, nothing abstract about that.

Earphones and vacuum cleaners notwithstanding, the mail issue would prove the most visceral in an age of technological innocence.


In 1975 Americans paid ten cents to mail a letter, their dime ensuring privacy protections first established in the 1878 Supreme Court decision *Ex parte Jackson.* But the average person didn't need to know case law to understand what *the sanctity of the mail* meant, or to understand, as a United States Postal Service slogan would later put it, *the mail matters.*

It mattered that a sealed envelope be left undisturbed, its contents revealed only to its recipient. It mattered that strangers weren't granted access to whatever might be inside.

Their grandparents had thought nothing of sharing early phone service with their *telephone neighbors,* several families on the same line able to listen in on everyone else's conversations. Nothing was private about that. *A party line is like a barn raising,* they were told, an appeal that made sense to a largely rural nation whose citizens depended upon and usually trusted one another. The invocation of civic virtue and sacrifice was meant to transform an inconvenience into a public service, if begrudgingly, human nature being what it was.

Some would later argue that monitoring the mail, while intrusive, was a small price to pay for safeguarding the nation's foreign and domestic security.

But notions of virtue and service were suspect to a post-Watergate population.

The Church Committee grilled former postmasters general who had run the Postal Service during the period in question. It wanted to know how high officials charged with a public trust could become functionaries, blindly executing unlawful policies on their watch. As it turned out, it was easy.

One postmaster insisted he had no inkling and would have halted the business immediately had he known. He took the sanctity of the mail seriously. His avowal heartened at least one committee member.

*If that attitude had prevailed, we would not have had a Watergate.*

A second postmaster staked out a more ambiguous position. He hadn't known, but only because he didn't want to know, even when the CIA director himself had tried to inform him.

*Mr. Dulles said that he wanted to tell me something very secret, and I said, "Do I have to know about it?"*

A committee member wanted to make sure he had heard the witness correctly.

*As I understand your testimony, you said you were told there was a secret, and you did not want to know what the secret was.*

That in itself seemed almost un-American. But the postmaster stood his ground.

*I felt it was up to the CIA to take care of what they had to do in the spying business.*

The committee also inquired into the mechanics of the operation. It must have been difficult to divert and process so much mail without anyone suspecting. Anyone, that is, who wasn't in the spying business.

Witnesses were happy to dive into the weeds, to the best of their ability.

The letters, once *filched* (a new term of art), were taken to a separate location and opened.

*How did you do it? Did you steam-kettle?*

The witness wasn't sure.

*I can only speculate that they used steam and other sophisticated devices in which they were trained.*

After being copied the letters were resealed and sent on their way, with almost no one the wiser.


Not every witness deplored the program. The former attorney general of the United States, John Mitchell, presented a vivid hypothetical to the committee for its consideration.

*Let me give you a hard one. We know that the Embassy of X has got an atomic bomb in its basement that it can put off in Washington, right down here, any time they want to.*

Would the committee, he wondered, really ask someone to get a warrant first, instead of running into the building right away?

One senator took up the challenge.

*No atomic bombs have been developed that you can put into an envelope. We are talking about mail here.*

Mitchell's argument would be known in time as *the ticking bomb scenario*, and would become a staple of the popular imagination. Americans didn't need to know that the idea was first broached in the early nineteenth century by an English philosopher; it was enough that they had seen rogue agent Jack Bauer in action on the TV show *24*, which was also a favorite of Washington insiders.

For the record, the committee noted that some CIA staffers were also unperturbed about the investigation. The CIA was routinely vilified *wherever there are bars and bowling alleys.* A significant swath of the country, all those folks on the bar stools, believed that the agency had killed Kennedy. They were always working themselves up over something.

*I wouldn't make a big hullabaloo about it.*

As the committee wound down it considered some thorny hypotheticals of its own.

It would be troubling if *President A*, in the future, were to politicize intelligence capabilities and target his own enemies; it might be worse if the agencies themselves again went rogue, as they already had, with no meaningful constraints or oversight.

*We cannot be certain what kinds of things may happen in this country.*

Executive overreach would need to be resisted and the rule of law restored.

Chairman Church closed with a warning delivered on national television. Like many other committee members, he had been shocked at the scale of the snooping. Powerful technologies existed that could monitor *messages that go through the air.* Everything— *telephone conversations, telegrams, it doesn't matter*—was subject to surveillance.

Even in 1975, it didn't take much to imagine the next step. Such awesome power could conceivably be turned on the American people themselves at any time.

*There would be no place to hide.*

The Church Committee findings spurred enactment of the Foreign Intelligence Surveillance Act of 1978. FISA, as it was called, would ensure strict oversight of intelligence operations through judicial review. The proceedings would be conducted in secrecy—*Need to know* only. Almost no one would need to know.

The reform was intended to end governmental surveillance abuses forever.

Church, like Louis Brandeis before him, would be spared the realization that his fears were well-founded, even dramatically understated, that NSA would someday capture trillions of transactions between billions of people with programs like *Total Information Awareness* and its derivatives. The goal, in the words of whistleblower William Binney: *to basically monitor the entire world.*

He knew. He had designed the systems to do it.

The challenge had been abstract, a question of mathematics, patterns, correlations, chains of connection, algorithmic inputs. He was stricken to watch as his talents put ordinary people in the grip of the government he had sworn to serve. Binney repudiated his work in 2001 and left the agency.

The systems kept functioning without him.

In the meantime, most people adjusted, those with nothing to hide as well as those who, given the choice, would probably rather not be noticed. The revelations of Edward Snowden simply confirmed what many had suspected: nothing was private anymore, and government was thoroughly intertwined with the corporate world.

In any case, it was probably an overreaction to give up Facebook or Google or Amazon.

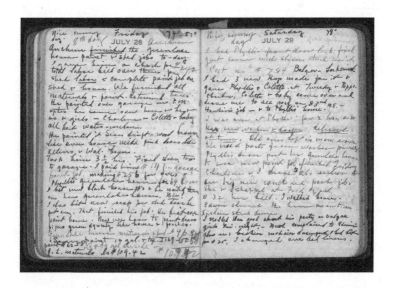

Diarists from the twenty-first century on (now *journaling* or *blogging*) would find themselves practicing an antiquated art, insisting, in the face of all evidence to the contrary, that disclosures could be voluntary, that the individual life could be separated out from the aggregate, that people weren't just data points.

That would be, in its way, an act of defiance.

*Statistics*

*It is sometimes said there are two kinds of people, number people and story people. Number people like to crunch data, the thinking goes, while story people like to work with words.*

*In the old days, number people would have carried slide rules in their pockets, along with ballpoint pens, and would have been easy to identify by the blue ink spot slowly spreading across a white shirt.*

*Story people, on the other hand, would favor pencils and might be seen scribbling in the margins of a paperback book.*

*Now we know that sometimes numbers tell stories, and sometimes stories need numbers, so the hard and fast divisions of the old days are no longer useful.*

*Maybe the trick is to become fluent in more than one language.*

I

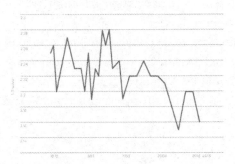

The figures tell the tale: the happiness score of average Americans has been in free fall since 1973. Fortunately, most of these folks can't read the chart and so don't know how bad their situation actually is. They lack the skill to interpret mathematical information (numbers, diagrams, graphs) in order to count, compute, measure, or model.

Accordingly, they can't make inferences from different strands of data.

That could make anyone unhappy.

In tests involving numbers, adult Americans perform *significantly below the average* worldwide, while Germans, Japanese, and Finns score significantly above average.

In other words, an alarming number of Americans are *innumerate*.

That's like being illiterate, but worse. Those who can't work with numbers in the twenty-first century will find themselves increasingly disadvantaged in a culture that prizes hard data over anecdote.

Occasionally articles attempt to convey the magnitude of the deficiency for a general readership. Disturbing scenarios are concocted: imagine not being able to split the bar tab, or not knowing what 15 percent off means, or not understanding that your boss has shaved eighteen minutes of overtime pay from every second shift for three weeks running.

To say nothing of not understanding compound interest, or what exponential growth rates of an infection across a population can mean for your own family.

You'd be at the mercy of anyone unscrupulous enough to exploit your incapacity.


Admittedly, not all data appears to be relevant at first glance.

Most people, for instance, don't care that s, the nineteenth letter of the alphabet, is the seventh most commonly used letter in English. It isn't something anyone necessarily wonders about.

But given a moment's thought, one starts to see s's everywhere; the snakelike sibilant seems ubiquitous, slithering into conversations, texts, DMs, and other social media spaces, while simultaneously appearing in stores, salons, song titles, sermons, sports, the census, and on all sorts of signs.

A society immersed in *S*'s: one would have to be sleepwalking not to see it.

Other statistical oddities also make sense once examined: instances of the name *Alexa* have fallen precipitously among new parents since Amazon introduced its digital assistant, dropping from thirty-second most popular name for newborns in 2015 to ninetieth place in just three years.

Maybe that's because an increasing number of families already have an Alexa at home.

But that's trivia, easy to dismiss, interesting but inconsequential.

It's harder to discount practical applications. Only someone who takes statistics seriously, for instance, has a real chance to win over a million dollars on *Jeopardy*.

Witness the winning strategy of 2019 *Jeopardy* champion James Holzhauer. He was a professional sports gambler from Las Vegas who had studied game theory and statistics before going on the show. His buzzer skills and encyclopedic knowledge contributed to his thirty-two-game winning streak, for sure, but it was his familiarity with statistical probabilities that helped him coast to victory over his competitors.

Take out the emotion, add the analysis, and watch the money roll in.

It's possible to construct a statistical picture of American life, a mosaic made from the 326 million people and 118,825,921 households across the country (the 552,830 persons who were homeless as of 2018 are, from a data-collection standpoint, all but invisible).

Such attempts are not entirely new.

The United States was once a fairly empty place; in 1790, there were just 4.5 residents per square mile, a number that had risen to 92.6 by 2018. We know that because the country's population density has been tracked in the census for over two hundred years. We know other things as well.

Americans are impatient: 48% of binge TV viewers in 2017 declared *I don't like waiting a week to find out what happens*. Viewers who binge-watched all eight seasons of *Game of Thrones* may have noticed that male characters spoke 75% of the time. Female characters spoke the most in season 7 (31% of the time).

Many Americans are superstitious: 13% believe that the number 13 is unlucky, while 22% knock on wood and 14% think a rabbit's foot brings good luck. 14% throw salt over their shoulder when necessary; 18% won't open an umbrella indoors, and 21% avoid walking under ladders when outside. 23% try extra hard not to break a mirror.

42% of adult Americans believe in ghosts; 65% believe in karma, *what goes around. comes around*; 47% believe that Lee Harvey Oswald did not act alone, 27% are convinced that the government is hiding aliens in Area 51, and 11% think the moon landing was faked.

22% contend that climate change is a hoax and no action need be taken to combat it. Which means that even more Americans may come to believe in karma in the future.


One can track finely targeted attitudes toward other elements of American life.

First dates: 25% of men and 31% of women are irritated by dates who *chew food very loudly*, while 70% of both men and women are bothered by dates who text during dinner; more men than women don't like dates who take pictures of food to post on social media, and 5% of men and 9% of women dislike dates who don't offer to split the bill (which means innumeracy can adversely affect one's social life).

Credit bureaus: 67% of Americans consider them *a necessary fact of life*, while 36% hate them more than the IRS, a level of intensity that can hardly be charted.

Cell phones: insurance vendors report that 13% of broken phones were damaged in one recent year when owners *spilled beer at sports events*, while another 12% were totaled when claimants, by their own admission, *threw device in anger*, possibly while looking up their FICO scores.

Print media: 47% of Americans would be *sad* if newspapers and magazines disappeared, but 1% would be *relieved*, the 1% possibly those who don't care to read any more articles about when the newest iPhone is coming out.

New Year's resolutions: 16% of Americans vowed in 2017 *to be a better person*, while 4% aimed simply *to enjoy life*, possibly by closing out their bank accounts and going off the grid.

Immigration: 75% of Millennials (born 1981–1996) think immigrants strengthen the country, while just 44% of the Silent Generation (1928–1945) think so; by 2100, when the number of deceased individuals on Facebook exceeds the living, both cohorts will be among the estimated 284 million North American *digital dead* whose opinions on the subject no longer matter.

Languages: 64% of Americans think *songs sound best when sung in English*, while 10% prefer to hum along in Italian. Norwegian and Spanish are among the easiest languages for English speakers to learn, requiring twenty-three intensive weeks to pick up; Mandarin, Arabic, and Japanese take forty-four weeks on average.

That's a Category 5 level of difficulty.

There are 41 million Americans who speak Spanish when home, while 1.2 million speak Arabic; 44% of Californians speak a language other than English at home.

And staying home may be advisable. Americans make 178 million trips every day over bridges deemed *structurally deficient* by engineers; it's especially dangerous to drive in Iowa, which leads the country in crumbling bridge infrastructure.

You're likelier to die from a dog attack than in a plane crash, particularly if you're a postal worker in California. If you have a tattoo, there's a 23% chance you already regret it. Baby Boomers buy twice as much wine as Millennials. If you like soft drinks, you may be one of the 5.97 billion consumers worldwide who bought a Coke in 2018 (known in the literature as *a purchase act*); you might also be among the 2.25 billion who bought Lay's potato chips while you were at it. Or spent $171 million on Reese's Pieces.

Which may partially explain why sales of women's plus-size apparel in the United States increased from $17 billion in 2013 to $20 billion in 2016.

It's clear from the data that people aren't just buying snacks. Americans spend 21.8% of their budget on health care and 18.8% on housing, which leaves little money for other needs. Perhaps not coincidentally, in 2016 over 307 billion discount coupons were distributed in the United States, of which 2.2 billion were redeemed, meaning at least 304.8 billion chances to save some loose change were lost.

Those with the means to travel left $960,105.49 at TSA airport checkpoints in 2018.

Across the country, there are 11,035 withdrawals from ATMs every minute.

Buyer's remorse sometimes sets in: on average, women have 41 items in their wardrobes they never wear, and online shoppers of all genders leave $7.6 million every minute in abandoned shopping carts.

That's a stat that might almost be considered melancholy.

Meanwhile, the U.S. birthrate in 2018 fell to the lowest level since the 1980s, which, if the drop continues, may eventually lead to a crisis in consumption.

Put another way: 1 million species are currently under threat of extinction worldwide, according to figures released in 2019, and the American consumer may yet be among them.


The most stressful jobs in America: enlisted military personnel, fire-fighters, airline pilots, taxi drivers, and event coordinators, who are tied with police officers. Which means anyone on active duty who flies to a wedding and takes a cab to a venue that burns down may blame the person who planned the event in the first place. And insist on an arrest.

Among the least stressful jobs: massage therapist, hair stylist, audiologist, and university professor (tenured). Which means priv-ileged academics can spend more time attending to personal quali-ty-of-life issues than to publishing.

The median full-time weekly earnings of American women av-erage just $708. Men earn more than women in the twenty most common occupations in the United States, whether truck drivers, salespersons, cooks, managers, customer service reps, software de-velopers, janitors, or accountants.

But sometimes individual women break free of demographic constraints and achieve their full potential.

Sonya Thomas held the women's record for the number of

hot dogs eaten in competition (45) until rival Miki Sudo raced ahead (48.5). According to statisticians at Nathan's Famous Hall of Fame, Thomas still holds the world record in competitive consumption of tater tots.

Winners of such contests receive as much as $10,000, which means that competitive eating could be lucrative if enough such opportunities were available.

At 98 pounds Thomas may never need plus-size womens wear, but her health-care costs, over time, could exceed the average.

Hot dogs reveal less about a culture than its consumption of hamburgers. The United States currently occupies fourth place on the Big Mac Index, just behind Switzerland, Norway, and Sweden. The index is widely considered a useful barometer of global purchasing power, the iconic burger a standardized commodity across the world.

Statistics also hint at darker trends in American life.

Income inequality in the United States, as of 2019, is at its greatest level since 1928 and the middle class continues to shrink, which means the buffer between haves and have-nots is now negligible.

If you lived in Boone, North Carolina, in 2012, you earned the lowest yearly income per capita in the country ($16,447).

If you lived in West Virginia in 2018, you were at ground zero of the opioid crisis, with the highest drug overdose death rate in the nation. Deaths in the state outnumbered births. 10,000 coal miners worked belowground and 2,935 on the surface. Over 70% of the population was designated either *overweight or obese*; 19.1% of the state's residents lived below the poverty line and 3,026 non-business bankruptcies were declared that year.

In Los Angeles 16,528 people lived in cars or other vehicles in 2019.

The gap between the median earnings of white households and black households in the United States is widening.

Best place to make a living in 2019: Wyoming.

Hate groups in America are flourishing, with 917 in 2016, up from 784 just two years earlier. The category is composed of a toxic mix of Skinheads, Anti-Muslims, Black Separatists, Neo-Nazis, Anti-LGBT, Neo-Confederates, and White Nationalists. The Southern Poverty Law Center, which has tracked such self-identifications for decades, is busier than ever.

One hundred active groups are classified simply as General Haters, a subcategory of angry people who are still shopping around.

Moments of national crisis like the COVID-19 contagion are tracked statistically as well.

As of April 2020, 39% of Americans wore face masks outside, a number that climbed to 66% by late May, while 46% cleaned their houses more during lockdown and 16% reduced their exercise regimes, the correlation between cleaning and exertion not clearly established.

The specter of food shortages worried 39% of the American public, while just 16% of Germans were similarly concerned.

The sale of hair clippers exploded by 352.6%, and the purchase of products for root touch-ups increased by 182.3%.

During a two-week period in March, retail sales of marijuana doubled in California.

By that time 70% of Americans had searched online for information about COVID, and 16% had contacted a medical professional through the Internet.

As of April 2020, 69% of Americans declared they would get a coronavirus vaccine if it became available, up from 48% in January.

Americans generate data from the moment they're first tagged with a Social Security number. Using social media, search engines, and e-commerce sites adds exponentially to the commodification of information.

Which means if you're driving on a bridge while humming in Italian and throwing salt over your shoulder or spilling beer on your cell phone or counting in Mandarin or clipping a coupon or hitting *save for later* in your shopping cart or watching YouTube re-creations of the moon landing or working the mines in West Virginia or joining a Neo-Neo-Something group while wearing a face mask, someone will know it.

The market for *data-driven decisions* has exploded and is currently being carved up by companies with the resources to aggregate disparate bits of data.

*We are the fact destination*, one company declares. *Data never sleeps*, a rival retorts, suggesting perhaps there's room enough for everybody in data analytics.

It's a mania that can now be monetized, if only by those who know their numbers.

## 2

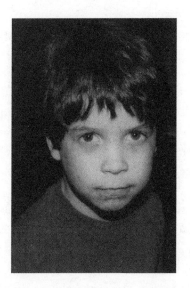

Every statistic can be unpacked so that the story at its heart emerges, like a lost language one has to relearn. It requires a rediscovery of the particular, the one-off, the ordinary.

As if anyone is really ordinary.

The year he was born, 1982, the most popular boy's name in America was Michael, followed by Christopher, Matthew, Jason, David, James, Joshua, and John.

His mother chose to call him Travis.

The year of his death, 2009, he would have had another 50.32 years of life left, on average, if he had been average.

He slipped away in his sleep of heart disease, the number one cause of death in America, aggravated by struggles with alcohol and depression, accounting in his own small way for the 69% increase in alcohol-related deaths among young people between 2007–2017.

He instantly became a member of the 27 Club, joining Jim and Janis and Kurt and Amy and everyone else who had abruptly passed away at the age of twenty-seven.

But the deeper truth, in his case, may be nonquantifiable.


There are no statistics for *death by broken heart*, the way a sensitive young man who loses his mother at the age of fourteen might never recover, though he carries her picture with him and kisses it every night, in whatever room or house or apartment he finds himself, the knowledge that he had once been cherished not enough to keep out the chill.

He might try to self-medicate as the years go by.

If his only access to health care is the emergency room, the last resort for someone without much money, he might become a regular of sorts, trying to survive.

He might even score a scarce and almost affordable spot in a re-hab facility, with the help of a frantic family, he might listen to talks about Twelve Steps, he might take two or three or four of them, he might leave with the best of intentions, he might try even harder to turn his life around.

But by that time, it might be too late.

The small-town cop summoned to the scene as a first responder took one look and sighed.

*Oh no, not him.*

Not the genial young man he had tried to help, more than once, not the kid who had seemed so embarrassed about needing that help.

The mothers of his school friends said the same thing at the memorial: *not him.*

Not the one who had shown so much promise, so much more than most of their own sons.

Twelve years earlier his mother had died at age fifty-one from breast cancer, one of the 28.2 per 100,000 women struck that year.

She was one of the 13% whose cancer hadn't been caught by a mammogram, though she had done her duty and been given the all-clear.

By the time her condition was discovered it was, they said, Stage IV. They told her there wasn't a Stage V.

No statistics can capture the shock of a diagnosis, the way a curt pronouncement from a doctor can cut straight through a situation, leaving questions like *why me, why now* echoing in one's head.

Her loved ones did what research they could. None of the sites were helpful in answering the only question they cared about: How long?

*Because statistics are based on large groups of people, they can-
not be used to predict exactly what will happen to an individual
patient.*

Statistics couldn't tell them she would never watch her children
grow up.


She didn't see her doctors very often in treatment, they were remote
and busy, but the nurses were wonderful. She liked their warmth.
There were no unspoken reproaches, no lectures about lifestyle
choices.

As a divorced single mother on public assistance who clipped
coupons and fed four children on food stamps, she had never had
much time to spend on herself.

Not much time to worry about not feeling well.

Not much time to find doctors who would accept her medical
coverage, or figure out how to buy the gas to get there.

She would probably not have wanted to be remembered for the
circumstances of her death, nor be defined by a demographic. She
had never liked abstractions.

She would rather have been remembered for all the other moments, the kind that arose from attention to family and friends.


Many of those moments revolved around her youngest son.

Once she stayed up till 4a.m. to put the finishing touches on
his school project. It had started off as a room for his hamster but
became more ambitious, under her direction, until it rose two stories to become a hamster condo, with black-and-white-checkered
flooring made out of contact paper and a spiral staircase fashioned
from toothpicks.

Chances are his teacher suspected something, but he got an *A* anyway.

He got another *A* for a book report he faked for an English class the year after her death, four pages concocting the plot, character development, conflicts, and revelations of a novel he titled *Twelve Shots*, the story of a bike messenger in a big city. It was faster to write the fake paper than read a real book.

*Cars were always honking and people were always getting mad at him. From Tom almost shooting a man on the subway to Tom almost being shot by a crazy lady getting out of her car, the plot was always revolving around the dangers of his job and guns. Tom was a guy who I could relate to, not always sure about himself, had some courage, and was overall a very nice guy. I didn't love the ending, but it was good enough to make me close the book with a smile.*

He fooled the teacher (*good job*) but he probably wouldn't have fooled her.


She knew the things they say only a mother knows, the kind of deep knowledge that disappears when those who possess it are gone.

She knew he hated bananas because they were slimy, but loved vegetable lo mein without the vegetables;

She knew he could never say good night just once, as a boy, he had to pop his head around the stairs two, three times, until she called out, for the second or third time, *Go to bed, Trav,* which seemed to satisfy him;

She knew he was afraid of the dogs on his paper route, especially the two little barkers, so she drove close to the curb at that house and let him stay in the car as he threw the paper wildly out the window, hoping it would land close enough;

She knew he had a sweetness that was special.

Who knows what else she would have learned about her son as he grew older.


She tried to encourage his interests. If he did his chores, he could spend his allowance on whatever he wanted.

He collected football cards and mounted them under plastic in a binder covered with NFL logos. He knew the players, the rankings, the weaknesses and strengths of each team he followed, especially his beloved Buffalo Bills. At one time he'd thought about becoming a sports statistician, or a play-by-play announcer, when that still seemed possible.

He excelled at analysis; he had never been never much of a player.

In Pop Warner baseball they put him in the outfield. A dreamer, he would stare up at the clouds or down at the grass, hands on knees, each separate blade seeming to deserve attention, as pop flys landed around him and teammates screamed *Trav!* to no avail.

Later, he liked it when his family came to his basketball games, though he was clear-eyed about his team's prospects.

*We suck*, he would say, but it was fun.

He liked to swim (she had made her children take lessons) and when he got older he would bodysurf in a wet suit off the cold Pacific coast of Northern California. In the ocean he could forget himself, not think too much about what he had lost.


She was studying for an associate degree as a medical assistant before she got sick. It was a job she would have been good at, the way she put people at ease. A stipend for $400 helped make it possible (*We hope this grant will provide valuable assistance to you in the pursuit of your educational goals*) and she could scrimp a little more while studying.

She had always been smart but was seriously sidetracked when the kids came. Now they could all do their homework together.

One of her classes required that she write an essay, a task she hadn't attempted in thirty years. She could have written about anything; she loved art (especially Klimt and O'Keeffe), she liked mysteries (Sue Grafton or Dean Koontz), she had once worked her way through much of Julia Child.

She chose to write about him.

The three-page piece, "A Thoughtful Son," was carefully outlined, the argument developed in stages (*First of all, furthermore, lastly*), the process not much different, really, than making a staircase from toothpicks. Once you got the idea, the rest was just execution.

*Thesis: Travis, my eleven-year-old son, has always been my most thoughtful child.*

*Point of Development: His consideration of strangers, friends and family, never ceases to amaze me.*

She bolstered her argument with examples: an elderly woman drops her purse in the supermarket and he picks up what she's spilled; a boy in a drugstore is short five cents at checkout, so he hands him a nickel; a little girl crashes her bike and starts to cry, so he gives her a LifeSaver and walks her home; a neighbor boy doesn't have many toys, so he gathers his own action figures and gives them away.

The evidence was mounting, but it wouldn't hurt to pile it on.

*Lastly:* he is close to his little sister, Devon, and sometimes plays with her, which makes her happy, and he gives his mother a hug when she's discouraged.

Case made, all that was left was the close.

*I can honestly say that I love each of my children equally, and I make a conscious effort to value their individual qualities. However, being a mother is an endlessly challenging, and sometimes unappreciated, job. Thankfully, Travis' kind and thoughtful nature makes that job a little easier.*

She didn't mention that the niceness hadn't come from nowhere, that her own neighbors had laughed when she told them she wanted to become a nicer person, because they didn't see how that was possible.

She also didn't say, because she could not have known, that the depression she struggled with throughout her life was something else they may have shared.

She died in the early hours of Easter Sunday.

That whole week they had watched the Great Comet of 1997, Hale-Bopp, as it streaked across the sky. It was hard not to see its appearance as a portent, a sign that the universe was paying its own homage to her.

The comet reached its point of maximum brightness just after she passed.

They liked to imagine it had picked her up before moving on.

Twelve years later his friends carved his initials, *TWM*, on a hillside above the school where they had been together years earlier. The

large letters could be seen for a while from the roads below until the
school district removed them.

For a few years afterwards family and friends gathered each August on the beach he had loved to remember him, until the enormity
of his death diminished and they moved into a life without him.

They told themselves he wasn't alone, not anymore.

*He's with her.*

*Snapshots*

*How does one hold on to the past? In the twenty-first century, those who don't write diaries or books might still take pictures, at last count over one trillion shots every minute. Few of the images in this digital deluge are looked at again. Nor are they printed, hung on a wall, or pasted carefully, with captions, to the pages of what used to be called a photo album.*

*They essentially disappear.*

*Apps like Snapchat embrace this ephemerality.*

*The term snapshot was first devised to convince an amateurish public that any moment quickly captured by a home camera—however unfocused or poorly composed—was memorable, that skill didn't matter as much as the act of memorializing itself. Generations grew up using Brownies, Instamatics, and Polaroids to save such Kodak moments. Their descendants now post images on Instagram.*

*Over the years, snapshot has acquired an ancillary meaning.*

*It has also come to connote an isolated observation, a stray thought, a perception that may be provisional, just as those early pictures were.*

*Snapshots, in this sense, mirror the fitful movements of memory.*

*Henry Ford's Childhood Home*

Henry Ford put a nation on the move, selling sixteen million Model Ts to average Americans in the early twentieth century, transforming a horse-and-buggy country into a car culture. For the first time families could afford to *take off* in a way that was unimaginable in earlier eras.

He is less well known for the creation of Greenfield Village, a part of the Henry Ford museum complex in Michigan. It features actual historical structures relocated from their original sites. A visitor can see Thomas Edison's laboratory, the Ohio home and bicycle shop of the Wright Brothers, and the Illinois courthouse where Abraham Lincoln practiced law. Visitors can also ride in a Model T and sit in the Rosa Parks bus.

The village is a theme park, showcasing—even fetishizing—the preservation of the American past.

One can tour the house that Ford himself was born in. He insisted that every detail be exactly as he remembered it, even as he also averred, more generally, that *everything is in flux*.

His business model, after all, was predicated upon resisting the impulse to stay put.

But there was something about the idea of rootedness that was profoundly important to this restless American.

**MODERN HOME No. 113**

FIRST FLOOR.                    SECOND FLOOR.

# $1,062.00

For $1,062.00 we will furnish all the material to build this Eight-Room House, consisting of Lumber, Lath, Shingles, Mill Work, Siding, Flooring, Ceiling, Finishing Lumber, Building Paper, Pipe, Gutter, Sash Weights, Hardware and Painting Material.

By allowing a fair price for labor, brick, cement and plaster, which we do not furnish, this house can be built for about $2,475.00, including all material and labor.

For Our Free Offer of Plans See Page 1.

A MODERN house with gambrel roof, large front porch, 22 feet by 6 feet 6 inches, and side porch 15x6 feet. The side entrance makes it very convenient for city or suburban residence or country home. The side porch could be very easily arranged to open up to a driveway which might be made directly at side of the house.

The rooms are very conveniently arranged with a large parlor or living room, 22 feet long by 13 feet wide, with a large reception hall, dining room and kitchen, and a nook in front of the reception hall. Three fair size bedrooms on the second floor and one large bedroom across the front, with a bay window, also bath room, size 7 feet by 13 feet. Five large closets on the second floor; one closet on the first floor. Inside cellar entrance leading from the side entry with rear stairs to the second floor from the dining room; also an outside cellar entrance.

We furnish our Windsor front door glazed with leaded glass. All interior doors for the first and second floors are of clear solid yellow pine, five-cross panel. Our Crystal leaded glass window for the large window in the parlor, hall, bay window in the dining room and bay window in the front bedroom of the second floor. All interior trim, such as baseboard, casing and molding, is clear yellow pine. Clear yellow pine flooring for entire house and for porches. Sided with cypress siding and roofed with cedar shingles.

Main open stairs are of unique pattern of clear plain sawed oak. Sufficient quantity of paint for two coats of exterior work. Varnish and wood filler for two coats of interior finish.

Excavated basement under the entire house, 7 feet 2 inches from floor to joists. Rooms on the first floor are 9 feet 2 inches from floor to ceiling; rooms on second floor, 8 feet from floor to ceiling.

**This house is 27 feet 6 inches wide by 40 feet long and can be built on a lot 37 feet wide.**

Complete Hot Air Heating Plant, for soft coal, extra.................... $ 95.06
Complete Hot Air Heating Plant, for hard coal, extra.................... 97.00
Complete Steam Heating Plant, extra.................................... 179.65
Complete Hot Water Heating Plant, extra................................ 220.62
Complete Plumbing Outfit, extra........................................ 133.10

SEARS, ROEBUCK                              CHICAGO,
AND CO.                                     ILLINOIS

*House in Sears Catalog*

For a time, given the new powers of mass production, Americans could buy an affordable house from the Sears catalog to accompany their affordable car from Ford. The prefabricated homes were shipped by rail for assembly on-site. Customers were advised to budget *a fair price for labor, brick, cement and plaster, which we do not furnish.*

70,000 such homes sold, many of them still standing today.

But assembling the shell of a home was just the first step. It would have to be furnished with the myriad items necessary to daily life—washing machine, drill bits, firearms, kitchen crockery—all available at Sears stores or through the company's mail order catalog.

Sears would eventually file for bankruptcy in 2018, reportedly *mired in debt and deserted by shoppers.*

No one knows how many of those shoppers kept their beloved catalogs, if only to put on eBay.

*The Doll Family House*

There's at least one notable American home that could never be prefabricated.

*23 rms, 7bds, 3bths, 1,300 handcrafted objects*—tiny porcelain tubs, books, plates made out of buttons, kittens and puppies that trot alongside the ten Doll children in the house. A turkey to be carved sits on a kitchen side table; a portrait of George Washington hangs in the parlor.

It's a fixer-upper that took fifty years to finish. The little girl who built it, Faith Bradford, grew into an old woman while tweaking her life's work.

Now it sits in the Smithsonian National Museum of American History, impervious to the shocks that have beset home ownership in the outer world, where more and more Americans cannot afford to buy.

Visitors invariably marvel at the scale of the house (*It's a mansion*).

But anyone with contact paper and wood can build a resplendent home for themselves, a world in miniature without a mortgage.

Meanwhile, in the Doll home, trunks and suitcases are piled in the attic, ready for a trip. But no one will likely ever leave this house.

Its tiny figures are suspended in time, and one suspects they might want it that way.

*The Kennedy Car, Henry Ford Museum*

During his lifetime Henry Ford acquired various *memento mori* of American life, like the rocker that Abraham Lincoln had been sitting in when he was shot. Ford museum officials after his death continued the tradition and eventually purchased the car in which President Kennedy had been killed.

One can almost imagine Jackie scrambling over the back of the Lincoln Continental.

The car sits next to vintage arches from an early McDonald's, two totems of national life placed in unlikely juxtaposition, like thoughts gathered in no particular order, or pictures tossed into a shoebox.

The curatorial impulse could be intentional. The language exists for such an organizational principle: *eclectic, motley, raggle-taggle.*

You might say it's a model of the mind itself in operation.

Ford would probably have approved; he was always interested in how things worked.

*Dealey Plaza, November 22, 1963*

Those who don't have the means to purchase life-size relics of the assassination can construct a scale model of Dealey Plaza, replete with a grassy knoll and, if they wish, a second shooter. It's history available to anyone who has a home workshop.

This particular iteration reflects the official version of the event. The wounded president is frozen in the defensive crouch made famous in the Zapruder film. The faces of the onlookers are featureless, caught just before the shock registers. A few are looking away.

The moment of national trauma is fixed forever, a ready point of reference for anyone who needs a reminder.

*Dealey Plaza, Texas School Book Depository in background*

Imagine if it were possible to change the past, to place the vulnerable president just outside the rifle's reach a moment before the gunfire rang out.

It would be an awesome power.

It would require a different way of thinking about history. One would need to be more flexible, less locked in to any one retelling of events.

Language itself would be altered. Phrases like *it's too late now* or *what can you do* could be retired; others, like *I give up* or *leave it alone,* might be used less often.

Such a power could be abused, certainly, and the logistics would be daunting.

But imagining a different way of being might be worth it, if only to keep the notion of possibility alive.

*Bus Wreck, 1941*

Sometimes it's a local calamity that gets all the attention, even while the world at large is engulfed in chaos.

Zoom in, and a cousin, friend, or neighbor is tossed around in a bus on a hillside close to home; zoom out, and strangers are swept up in tumultuous events that seem utterly remote.

The abrupt shifts in perspective can be dizzying.

It's a question of how much one can hold in one's head.

*Toy Soldiers, Battle of Saratoga, West Point Museum*

In the diorama the Continental Army is advancing against the British, early in the engagement that will end in victory for the ragtag American forces.

The battle has already ended for one fallen Redcoat, while another slumps to his knees nearby.

The outcome will mark a turning point in the American Revolution, worthy of study by future generations of American military. Even to civilians, the tactical lesson is clear; the tight formation of the British troops seems ill-advised against the looser, more nimble Americans.

Of course, it could have gone another way, with the colonials faltering, even turning and running in retreat.

But moments like that are less likely to be memorialized in national museums.

*Field where General Reynolds fell, Gettysburg*

To the nineteenth-century photographer the focal point of the picture is the grassy area up center, the now empty space where Union general John F. Reynolds was shot off his horse during the Battle of Gettysburg. His body has already been carried off, as befits a person of such rank.

The picture is captioned *Field where General Reynolds fell*. It's meant to mark absence.

But to a modern eye the field is full, bodies strewn in plain sight, blood-soaked shirts covering bloated chests. These men have fallen too, but like cannon fodder, littering the field, left to lie in the sun. Their stories will never be told.

It's the Great Man Theory of History: a favored few are accorded capital letters while the rest, nameless, lead lowercase lives.

ROADS · KENNETH J ELLINGTON · ROBERT A FULKERSON · CHRISTIAN G G
AYMOND A GRAY · IVAN I GREEN · ISMAEL F HORNELAS · EDWARD M KACH
ORVILLE L KNIGHT · KEITH N MILLER · JAMES R O'BANION · JOSEPH M ORL(
ORTA · ROBERT M RASMUSSEN · ROLAND A RICHARD · CHARLES C DICKERS
Z · LARRY D SIMPSON · GERRAL A SMITH · WILLIAM O STEED · TOWNSER ST
TATE · VINCENT A TAYLOR · JAMES M TRUELOVE · CARL R VANN · JOHN E WA
· STEPHEN D WILKINSON · LEON WILSON · JAMES H ADAMS · JAMES G BUN
OWN · ROGER BROWN · RONALD C CONLEY · GARY L CROSS · DAVID R CR(
RODNEY T FUKUNAGA · NATHANIEL HUDSON · BRUCE T KING · THOMAS E L
AM L OVERSTREET · DANNY L PATRICK · ROBERT A PORTE · MICHAEL J VERHA
E ARREDONDO · WILLIAM F BAGGS Jr · JOHN T BOONE · STEPHEN J BORYSZE
GE A F DASHO Jr · WILLIAM J DAUBERT · GERALD A DECKER · DWIGHT M DUF
RANDALL L HAWK · WILLIAM A HERING · THOMAS E HOFER · THOMAS J HUC
S KEITH · RONALD S ROSSINI · MICHAEL W LIZARRAGA · THOMAS G MANDEF
JOHN L MORGAN Jr · STEVEN L McFARLAND · JOHN G NURSE · STANLEY J OT
IE LEE RATCLIFF · OLIVER E REYNOLDS Jr · LOEL F LARGENT · JOSEPH F SPINNI(
D J TOWARD · EUGENE C ZAMORA · JOHNNIE LEE ANDERSON · EMMONS E FU
URIE E BARNES · BEVERLY L BARNHART · DONALD C BOSBERY · KENNETH E BR(
EDWARD V EIDEN Jr · NEIL P FARMER · GUY T FLETCHER Jr · RICHARD D AUSBR(
RUCE D HENDERSON · RICHARD E HUFF · ROBERT L KNIGHT Jr · ANDREW M KU
EPHEN M LEWIS · MICHAEL E MATTA · GONZALO H VILLASENOR · DALE L MILBR
ILLS · WILLIAM L OWEN Jr · JOSEPH FLAVIO PAEZ · CLIFTON D POTTS · PETER E RE
WRENCE E ZAPOLSKI · ROBERT L SCHEIDEL Jr · ROBERT H SMART · MATTHEW E SN
E M SOURS · PETER L STITH · LARRY T TURNER · CHARLES H MEEKS Jr · ALFRED WE
DONALD S SAWYER · STAMATIOS G ALEXANDER Jr · SA ATUATASI Jr · PATRICK E BL,
Y D CHANDLER · BERNHARD M CHRISTIANSEN · DUANE R DAVIS · ERNEST L DE S(
ALDERON · DONALD G DROZ · JEFFERY S DYER · STEPHEN M FRY · FREDRICK M H
WAY · DANNY W HOULE · CLAUDE T JENKINS · CORBIN C TINDALL · MARYUS N JO
NG · ROBERT C KING · ARNOLD W LAMP Jr · RICHARD K LEMMON · JOHN C LEONA
R L PRITCHARD Jr · DONALD G RESPECKI · MICHAEL L SMITH · THOMAS H ROBERTS
N · SYLVESTER V SEKNE · MANUEL A RIVERA-DELVALLE · ROBERT T SMITH · JOHN THI
O E JONES · MILES D TOUCHBERRY Jr · JERRY G WEATHERFORD · STEVEN E WETTERGR
R · ELROY WILSON · LOREN E WOOD Jr · CURTIS S WOODS · ROBERT L WORTHINGT(
N Jr · LUTHER E BALL Jr · LARRY B BARFIELD · RICHARD I BRENNER · ROBERT J BRINKM,
III · HARRY P BURTON · LOUIS CASTRO · IRVING S CHENOWETH III · ARLIE RAY COLLI
DASHER · DAVID F DECKER · BOBBY LEE DENTON · GARY G DETRICK · GLENN W DON
· HAROLD L GREEVER · TERRY L GUMP · RICARDO IBRAHIN ROMERO · ROGER W HO(
OWARD · HAROLD N JENSEN · KENNETH V JENSEN · BRUCE E JOHNSON · TERRY E JON
EDFORD Jr · JAMES O LYNCH · JOSEPH D MACY · LARRY C MARTIN · WILLIAM H MARTZ
Jr · JOSEPH D MELONSON Jr · RALPH D McMURTRY · DAVID T NELSON · JOSEPH A ORET
JOSEPH J REMEIKAS Jr · RICHARD A BROWNE · LARRY O ROBBINS · THOMAS G ROMAIN
SCHMELZLE · WILFRED F SCHMIDT Jr · CHRISTOPHER L SENESE · NELSON O VAN HOUTE
RHEIM · RONALD H YOUNG · ROYCE H ADAMS · JAMES N BLAVAT · MICHAEL R BURNETI
· MICHAEL K NICKERSON · JAMES W DEAN · FRANCIS E DUNLAP Jr · ROBERT M GENDRON
RETH · VICTOR M HODSON · MICHAEL D HOLMES · GARY O JACOBS · ANDREW E JENKIN
FRANCISCO LICON · JAMES W MOORE Jr · ALEXANDER D NEIBAUER · CHARLES D CROSBY
PORTER · LLOYD D QUILLEN · THEODORE F SIEGEL · THOMAS M SMITH · WILLIAM L SPER
B TUTEN · MICHAEL N VITA

*Vietnam Veterans Memorial*

58,320 names are inscribed on the stark stone slabs of the Vietnam Veterans Memorial on the National Mall. *BOBBY LEE, GARY, RICARDO, NEIL, ROBERT*—the simple procession is strangely powerful in its specificity.

The black surface is reflective; onlookers are pulled into the picture if they get close enough, but the names, etched in white, are more sharply delineated.

That keeps the focus where it arguably ought to be.

*Woolworth's Lunch Counter, 1960*

Not all national struggles have been fought on formal battlefields; some have taken place in ordinary spaces across the country, like the bridges, town squares, and dime stores marking important sites in the civil rights movement of the 1960s.

Four empty seats from a lunch counter are now showcased in the Smithsonian, mundane objects transformed into iconic relics of resistance.

They commemorate the moment in Greensboro, North Carolina, when students of color, denied service, sat at the counter and refused to leave. The *sit-ins* would spark a national movement that resounded across the decade.

And now visitors can imagine themselves in the seats, wondering, *What would I have done?*

*Deer at Attention, Somewhere in Alaska*

## USAGov's Guide to Displaying the American Flag

You can display the flag outside from sunrise to sunset. If you want to fly it after dark, it will need to be lit. Don't fly the flag during inclement weather, unless it's an all-weather flag.

Store your flag in a well-ventilated area. If it gets wet, make sure it's completely dry before storing it. If the flag is damaged or worn out, it should be burned and disposed of with dignity.

The flag's 13 alternating red and white stripes represent the 13 original colonies. Its 50 white stars on a blue field represent the 50 states.
The colors on the flag represent:
- Red: valor and bravery
- White: purity and innocence
- Blue: vigilance, perseverance, and justice

朕深ク世界ノ大勢ト帝國ノ現狀トニ鑑ミ非常ノ措置ヲ以テ時局ヲ收拾セムト欲シ茲ニ忠良ナル爾臣民ニ告ク

朕ハ帝國政府ヲシテ米英支蘇四國ニ對シ其ノ共同宣言ヲ受諾スル旨通告セシメタリ

抑々帝國臣民ノ康寧ヲ圖リ萬邦共榮ノ樂ヲ偕ニスルハ皇祖皇宗ノ遺範ニシテ朕ノ拳々措カサル所曩ニ米英二國ニ宣戰セル所以モ亦實ニ帝國ノ自存ト東亞ノ安定トヲ庶幾スルニ出テ他國ノ主權ヲ排シ領土ヲ侵スカ如キハ固ヨリ朕カ志ニアラス然ルニ交戰已ニ四歳ヲ閲シ朕カ陸海將兵ノ勇戰朕カ百僚有司ノ勵精朕カ一億衆庶ノ奉公各々最善ヲ盡セルニ拘ラス戰局必スシモ好轉セス世界ノ大勢亦我ニ利アラス加之敵ハ新ニ殘虐ナル爆彈ヲ使用シテ頻ニ無辜ヲ殺傷シ慘害ノ及フ所眞ニ測ルヘカラサルニ至ル而モ尚交戰ヲ繼續セムカ終ニ我カ民族ノ滅亡ヲ招來スルノミナラス延テ人類ノ文明ヲモ破却スヘシ斯ノ如クムハ朕何ヲ以テカ億兆ノ赤子ヲ保シ皇祖皇宗ノ神靈ニ謝セムヤ是レ朕カ帝國政府ヲシテ共同宣言ニ應セシムルニ至レル所以ナリ

朕ハ帝國ト共ニ終始東亞ノ解放ニ協力セル諸盟邦ニ對シ遺憾ノ意ヲ表セサルヲ得ス帝國臣民ニシテ戰陣ニ死シ職域ニ殉シ非命ニ斃レタル者及其ノ遺族ニ想ヲ致セハ五内爲ニ裂ク且戰傷ヲ負ヒ災禍ヲ蒙リ家業ヲ失ヒタル者ノ厚生ニ至リテハ朕ノ深ク軫念スル所ナリ惟フニ今後帝國ノ受クヘキ苦難ハ固ヨリ尋常ニアラス爾臣民ノ衷情モ朕善ク之ヲ知ル然レトモ朕ハ時運ノ趨ク所堪ヘ難キヲ堪ヘ忍ヒ難キヲ忍ヒ以テ萬世ノ爲ニ太平ヲ開カムト欲ス

朕ハ茲ニ國體ヲ護持シ得テ忠良ナル爾臣民ノ赤誠ニ信倚シ常ニ爾臣民ト共ニ在リ若シ夫レ情ノ激スル所濫ニ事端ヲ滋クシ或ハ同胞排擠互ニ時局ヲ亂リ爲ニ大道ヲ誤リ信義ヲ世界ニ失フカ如キハ朕最モ之ヲ戒ム宜シク舉國一家子孫相傳ヘ確ク神州ノ不滅ヲ信シ任重クシテ道遠キヲ念ヒ總力ヲ將來ノ建設ニ傾ケ道義ヲ篤クシ志操ヲ鞏クシ誓テ國體ノ精華ヲ發揚シ世界ノ進運ニ後レサラムコトヲ期スヘシ爾臣民其レ克ク朕カ意ヲ體セヨ

御名御璽

昭和二十年八月十四日

裕仁
御璽

内閣總理大臣男爵 鈴木貫太郎
海軍大臣 米内光政
司法大臣 松阪廣政
陸軍大臣 阿南惟幾
軍需大臣 豐田貞次郎
厚生大臣 岡田忠彦
國務大臣 櫻井兵五郎
國務大臣 左近司政三
國務大臣 下村宏
大藏大臣 廣瀬豐作
文部大臣 太田耕造
農商大臣 石黒忠篤
外務大臣兼大東亞大臣 東郷茂德
内務大臣 安倍源基
運輸大臣 小日山直登

*The Emperor Speaks*

The neat brushstrokes represent complete capitulation, the Empire of Japan ordered by its emperor to surrender to allied forces after a second Japanese city had been destroyed by the A-bomb.

But few would believe a printed declaration, even one stamped with the Imperial Seal. Few would trust that the war fought in the emperor's name was over until he himself told them.

And so he spoke.

The speech was recorded and broadcast at noon on August 15, 1945.

No ordinary person had heard the voice of the godlike emperor. But no ordinary person had contemplated *the total extinction of human civilization*, a specter the emperor now raised with his subjects.

The original recording was never played again.

But the Allies had made a copy, and now anyone can listen to the tremulous declaration on the Web.

*Seeing Used to Be Believing*

Looking at pictures was once uncomplicated; photographs reflected what most people considered a recognizable version of reality. Now digital capabilities allow even the most unsophisticated shooter to alter an image, move something around, add an element, airbrush a face. And such trickery has moved far beyond the still image.

Video and auditory material can be manipulated to put words in anyone's mouth. Even an emperor can't necessarily be trusted now.

There's a new word for it: *Deepfakes.*

Viewers have to make up their own minds, decide what's real and what's not, mull over sources and motives, guard against deception.

Sometimes, it's easier not to worry about it.

*Traveling Back in Time*

What if you found yourself returning for the first time to the little town you had left sixty years earlier?

You wouldn't be interested in what had changed; you'd want to see if anything was still the same. But it might be difficult to communicate with the locals.

You'd need to translate for the younger folk, explain what *turn back the clock* meant to those who had never seen a timepiece with a dial.

Other phrases from the unfamiliar idioms of your youth: *roll down the window, hold your horses, like a broken record, somebody get the phone.*

The effort to reach out might be rewarding.

For some of the kids it would be revelatory, as if their history books had come alive.

*Everyone Loves a Parade*

What if the whole town came out to fete you, held a parade in your honor, gathered to welcome the prodigal back?

It would be quite a party.

Bands, barbecue, toddlers held aloft, sodas on Main Street, all the trappings of small town life you remembered as if it were yesterday.

All you would have to do was close your eyes to see it.

*You Can't Go Home Again*

In the end, after the trip was over, you would realize that the place you had wanted to visit exists only in memory.

You wouldn't come back.

Even if you had a son named Jimmy who liked to take pictures and offered to do all the driving.

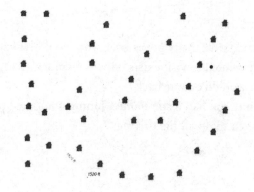

*Campfire Structure Status, Paradise, California*

The tiny houses on the CAL FIRE chart are arrayed like Monopoly markers, each a representation of a home that's been destroyed in the worst fire in California history. The online site has been prepared for survivors, residents who fled the conflagration and want to know whether they have anything to come back to.

It's interactive, but that feature isn't much use in this instance. Move the cursor, and a neighborhood is gone; zoom farther out and the whole town is a wash of black, 18,000 structures wiped away in a local apocalypse.

It's not a map of what is anymore, it's a map of what was, just a few hours earlier.

Most of the time we hardly notice, but it's striking how quickly the past becomes an abstraction.

*Burnt-Out Lot, Paradise, California*

The young man is standing at the place where he once rented a home, now just a black dot on a CAL FIRE chart. It's mesmerizing, really, worse than the worst thing he could have imagined. The chimney still stands, but the rest of his stuff, *everything I had*, has been reduced to rubble. Even his cast-iron skillet has melted from the force of the fire.

That's one heirloom that won't be passed on to the next generation.

He's got decisions to make. He can't stay, not here, he'll have to move on to another place, another town like Paradise, where he can start over. He's got time, that's what they tell him.

But the very idea of starting over exhausts him.

It's easier, for the moment, just to look at the ghostly remnants of the life he used to live.

*He's With Her*

It's a simple shot, taken on a day trip early in her illness when she was feeling good. She had always shied away from a camera, to the point where only a few images of her throughout the years could be found, but she knew her family would want something going forward, something to hold on to, so she let the picture be taken.

If it were up to her, she would have been happy just to pass on the moments that couldn't be captured on camera, the ones that would inspire the stories they might tell one another much later.

She came up with the ending to her own story after a long silence one day.

*I've had a good life. It's been a hard life, but I've been loved.*

*An American Family, 1903*

The formal portrait depicts a Minnesota shopkeeper's family, dressed in their Sunday best, at its center a three-year-old who has the whole of the twentieth century ahead of her.

A descendant of Irish immigrants, she has inherited a presumption that almost anything is possible.

She has no inkling, yet, that she will one day meet a young man, the love of her life, and shortly thereafter become a Gold Star widow in the First World War, and a Gold Star mother after the Second, losing their only child to tropical diseases that can't yet be cured in the 1950s. She will know something about the fearsome power of disease by then, having survived the Pandemic of 1918, but she won't know how to protect her son.

Nor does she know that her granddaughter, named after her husband, will one day write a book and put the three-year-old's picture in it, along with a shot of the grandfather she never knew.

Like most three-year-olds she probably wants to play, but on this occasion she has to sit still.

There will be time enough to ease into the tangled future that awaits her.

*A Fleeting Moment*

They were happy once, before the war, they probably made the kinds of plans that young people think will last forever.

They spent a brief time together and then it was over, all the plans in the world not enough to keep them safe from the hazards of history.

Years later, she wrote her son somewhere in the South Pacific: *Your father would be so proud of you, you know he was your age in the last war and he would now be 45 years old.*

When she lost him, she stopped writing letters for a very long time.

But she typed out a poem and probably read it over in many dark moods.

*Let fate do her worst, there are moments of joy,*
*bright dreams of the past which she cannot destroy . . .*

*An American Family, 1950s*

I sometimes study a picture of my family taken in the early 1950s, a candid shot in which no one is looking into or even seems to be aware of the camera. My mother crouches in the foreground, holding a camera of her own which she has aimed at something unseen that lies off to the side; my father stands farther back, hands on hips, his gaze following hers; my sisters stare off in opposite directions, oblivious to whatever it is that has drawn the interest of the grown-ups, and a fifth figure stands just out of sight, taking this picture of someone taking a picture, capturing four figures whose glances radiate outward beyond the fixed edges of the frame.

It's possible my mother is taking a picture of my brother and me, the babies, but I can't be sure.

Because I cannot tell what kind of event is being recorded—who took the shot, or why—and because it is impossible to determine what anyone in the picture is actually looking at, the image seems oddly unmoored, with nothing to hold it in place.

I do know that the little girl in white shorts will one day pose for a picture by a lake.

The other little girl will have a son whose house burns down in a place called Paradise.

Both will be comforted in years to come by an uncle named Jimmy.

But for now, they're absorbed in the moment at hand.

Soon my father will be dead, though no one in the picture knows that; the house he remodeled for his young family will be razed to make room for a freeway; the postwar stability of the 1950s will shift into the unsettled '60s, and a nation's story will continue to be crafted from millions of such ephemeral moments.

No one in the picture knows that either.

The more I study this snapshot, the more I see an image on the verge of vanishing.

# POSTSCRIPT

*No one who has lived long enough exists only in the moment. Perhaps memories begin to form, in some fashion, shortly after birth, so that even a child has an intuition of what used to be.*

*In that case, one could spend a lifetime looking back.*

*Soon enough we learn that past and present are interwoven in ways that can sometimes surprise us, even as our lives are more thoroughly documented with each passing day.*

*We can still be struck by the unbidden recollection, the unexpected connection, the leap that can't yet be triggered by an algorithm.*

*Maybe the challenge is to preserve that capacity for surprise, to keep memory alive, then pass that power along to those who follow.*

*It will require a lifelong commitment.*

*And we may never know how the story ends, but, in time, someone else will.*

# Selected Photo Credits

## Shooters

## Soldiers

## *Secrets*

## *Statistics*

## *Snapshots*

of Political Materials, W.R. Poage Legislative Library, Baylor University

188  Bus wreck 1941: Colette Brooks
190  Toy soldiers diorama: Colette Brooks
192  Bodies at Gettysburg: Timothy O'Sullivan and Alexander Gardner, Library of Congress Prints and Photographs Division
194  Vietnam Memorial: Colette Brooks
196  Woolworth's lunch counter: Colette Brooks
198  Deer in Alaska: Colette Brooks
202  UFO sighting: Colette Brooks
204  Kansas welcome: James Nelson
206  Small town parade: James Nelson
208  Kansas farewell: James Nelson
210  Camp Fire graphic: Cal Fire
212  Burnt out lot, Paradise: Cory Rantanen
214  Charlene at lake: Colette Brooks
216  American family, 1903: Colette Brooks
218  Charlotte and Russell Brooks: Colette Russelle Brooks
220  American family, 1950s: Colette Brooks

# Acknowledgments

First of all, I owe a great debt to two friends and colleagues, Cecilia Rubino and Victoria Abrash, who offered encouragement and incisive feedback from the moment this book began to take shape. Thanks also to Abigail Franklin, another friend, for her support. The New School and Lang College provided faculty research funds, and Dean Stephanie Browner was always helpful. Along the way I was ably assisted by various students, among them Elisabeth Smith and Jesse Ludington. Thanks to Anomie Williams and Will Lucas for their skillful preparation of images, and LTI/Lightside for its work. The artists' community of Yaddo offered an inspired place to write a portion of the manuscript.

I drew upon several sources for supplementary materials, including Statista, the Department of Labor, the United States Census Bureau, the Congressional Record, the Centers for Disease Control, and reports published by the FBI and the Danbury, Connecticut, State Attorney's office. The Henry Ford museum in Michigan and the Smithsonian Museum in Washington, D.C., were rich repositories of national artifacts.

I am thankful for the friendship of my late colleague Robin Mookerjee, who had a profound appreciation for all things quirky.

My uncle, James Nelson, passed on his wartime scrapbook in hopes that I would someday tell his story and I have done so here, along with that of my sister, Charlene Brooks, and her son Travis, my nephew. Kirk Mulligan, Trav's father, gave me some material for that sequence. I want to thank my sister Diane Brooks for her encouragement and unwavering belief that family stories can illuminate something larger.

I am deeply indebted to my agent, Georges Borchardt, my publisher, Jack Shoemaker, and Counterpoint Press for making this book possible.

Lastly, I wish to dedicate this book to my grandmother, Charlotte French Brooks, who taught me to hold on to the moments, and to my niece Devon, for whom I hope to do the same.

© Will Lucas

COLETTE BROOKS has published two books and many literary essays. Her first book, *In the City: Random Acts of Awareness*, won a PEN/Jerard Fund Award as a distinguished work of nonfiction. Her second book, *Lost in Wonder: Imagining Science and Other Mysteries*, was a finalist for the Grub Street National Book Prize in Non-Fiction. Find out more at colette-brooks.com.